PENGUIN POPULAR REFERENCE

SPANISH PHRASE BOOK

SECOND EDITION

María Victoria Alvarez and
Jill Norman

Spanish Phrase Book

PENGUIN BOOKS

Published by the Penguin Group
Penguin Books Ltd, 80 Strand, London WC2R ORL, England
Penguin Putnam Inc., 375 Hudson Street, New York, New York 10014, USA
Penguin Books Australia Ltd, Ringwood, Victoria, Australia
Penguin Books Canada Ltd, 10 Alcorn Avenue, Toronto, Ontario, Canada M4V 3B2
Penguin Books India (P) Ltd, 11 Community Centre, Panchsheel Park,
New Delhi – 110 017, India
Penguin Books (NZ) Ltd, Cnr Rosedale and Airborne Roads, Albany, Auckland,
New Zealand
Penguin Books (South Africa) (Pty) Ltd, 24 Sturdee Avenue, Rosebank 2196, South
Africa

Penguin Books Ltd, Registered Offices: 80 Strand, London WC2R ORL, England

www.penguin.com

First published 1968
Second edition 1978
12

Printed in England by Cox & Wyman Ltd, Reading, Berkshire

Contents

6 Contents

8 Contents

Introduction

In this series of phrase books only those words and phrases that are essential to the traveller have been included. For easy reference the phrases are divided into several sections, each one dealing with a different situation.

   * Some of the Spanish phrases are marked with an asterisk – these attempt to give an indication of the kind of reply you may get to your questions and of questions you may be asked.

   At the end of the book is an extensive vocabulary list and here a pronunciation guide is given for each word. In addition there is an explanation of Spanish pronunciation at the beginning of the book and a brief survey of the essential points of grammar. It would be advisable to read these sections before starting to use the book.

For those who would like to study the phrases and perfect their pronunciation, a further aid is available in the form of two 90-minute cassettes which contain all the words and phrases spoken clearly and distinctly by Spanish men and women.

   A leaflet giving full details is available from The Institute of Tape Learning, P.O. Box 4, Hemel Hempstead, Herts HP3 8BT (tel. 0442 68484).

Pronunciation

The pronunciation guide is intended for people with no knowledge of Spanish. As far as possible the system is based on English pronunciation. This means that complete accuracy may sometimes be lost for the sake of simplicity, but the reader should be able to understand Spanish pronunciation, and make himself understood, if he reads this section carefully. In addition, each word in the vocabulary is given with a pronunciation guide.

VOWELS

All Spanish vowel sounds are pure, they are not slurred as in English. Final **e** is always pronounced.

Pronounce **a** as **a** in father	Symbol **a**	e.g. casa – house (ka-sa)
	e as **e** in bed	Symbol **e**	e.g. negro – black (ne-gro)
and	as **ai** in air	Symbol **ai, ay**	e.g. poder – to be able (po-dair)
	i as **i** in machine	Symbol **ee**	e.g. fin – end (feen)
	o as **o** in porter	Symbol **o(h)**	e.g. todo – all (toh-doh)

u as oo in boot   Symbol oo   e.g. mucho – much
(moo-cho)

COMPOUND VOWELS

In the groups ia, ie, io the i sound resembles y in yes	Symbol y, ee	e.g. alguien – anyone (alg-yen)
In the groups ue, ui, uo the u sound resembles w as in wet	Symbol w, oo	e.g. bueno – good (bwe-no).

CONSONANTS

Many are similar to English consonants but note the following:

c before e or i is pronounced th as in thin	Symbol th	e.g. cerrar – to shu (ther-rar)
c before a, o, u or a consonant is pronounced k	Symbol k	e.g. coche – car (ko-che)
final d is not always pronounced		e.g. edad – age (ai–da
g before e or i is pronounced like English h (hot) or Scottish ch (loch)	Symbol h	e.g. gente – people (hen-te)
g before a, o, u or a consonant is pronounced g as in got	Symbol g	e.g. gafas – glasses (ga-fas)
h is always silent		
j is like English h (hot) or Scottish ch (loch)	Symbol h	e.g. mujer – woman (moo-hair)
ll is like lli in million	Symbol lly	e.g. llamar – to call (llya-mar)

ñ is like **ni** in onion   Symbol **ny**   e.g. mañana – morning
(ma-nya-na)

q(u) is pronounced as **k**   Symbol **k**   e.g. queso – cheese
(ke-so)

r is trilled, **rr** trilled even more strongly

v is pronounced as **b**   Symbol **b**   e.g. vaso – glass
(ba-so)

z is pronounced **th** as in thin   Symbol **th**   e.g. manzana – apple
(man-tha-na)

This is the pronunciation used in Spain. In Spanish America there are one or two differences, notably c + e or i and z are pronounced s not th.

STRESS

Words ending in a vowel, **n** or **s** are stressed on the last syllable but one: ca**sa**, **ga**fas, **ven**den.

Words ending in a consonant other than **n** or **s** are stressed on the last syllable: hab**lar**, espa**ñol**.

Exceptions to these rules are indicated by a written accent: café, autobús, estación. In the pronunciation guide, words with irregular stress have the stressed syllable printed in bold.

Basic grammar

NOUNS

Nouns in Spanish are either masculine or feminine.
Nouns denoting males are masculine, as are most nouns ending in **–o**.
Nouns denoting females are feminine, as are most nouns ending in **–a**.

   e.g. tío – uncle; vaso – glass; tía – aunt; playa – beach.

Plural

The plural is formed by adding **–s** if the word ends in a vowel;
–es if it ends in a consonant.

   e.g. peseta – pesetas; tren (train) – trenes.

DEFINITE ARTICLE – the

el before a masculine singular noun	el banco (the bank)
los before a masculine plural noun	los bancos
la before a feminine singular noun	la peseta
las before a feminine plural noun	las pesetas

INDEFINITE ARTICLE – a, an

un before a masculine singular noun   un banco
una before a feminine singular noun   una peseta

ADJECTIVES

Adjectives agree in number and gender with the noun.
Those ending in **-o** change to **-a** in the feminine.
    e.g. fresco – fresca (fresh, cool).
Those ending in **-e** and most of those ending in a consonant are the
same in the masculine and the feminine.
    e.g. el coche grande; la casa grande.

The plural is formed by adding **-s** if the word ends in a vowel, **-es** if
it ends in a consonant.
    e.g. fresco – frescos; azul (blue) – azules.

The comparative and superlative are formed by putting **más** before
the adjective.
    e.g. un hotel barato   a cheap hotel
        un hotel más barato   a cheaper hotel
        el hotel más barato de la ciudad   the cheapest hotel in the town

POSSESSIVE ADJECTIVES

	s	*pl*
my	mi	mis
your (*familiar*)	tu	tus
his, her	su	sus
their, your (*polite*)	su	sus
our	nuestro	nuestros
your (*familiar*)	vuestro	vuestros

These adjectives agree with the thing possessed, e.g. mi casa (my house); mis casas (my houses); vuestro libro (your book); vuestra carta (your letter).

PERSONAL PRONOUNS

	subject	*object*
I	yo	me
you (*familiar*)	tú	te
you (*polite*)	usted	le (*m*), la (*f*)
he	él	le
she	ella	la
it	él/ella	lo
we	nosotros/-as	nos
you (*familiar*)	vosotros/-as	os
you (*polite*)	ustedes	los (*m*), las (*f*)
they *m*	ellos	los
they *f*	ellas	las

Personal pronouns are usually omitted before the verb.
  e.g. voy – I go; viene – he (she) comes.

Direct object pronouns are usually placed before the verb.
  e.g. me ve – he sees me.

Indirect object pronouns are the same as direct object pronouns except that **le** is used to mean to him, to her, to it, to you (*polite*), and **les** means to them and to you (*polite*). If a direct and an indirect object pronoun are used together, the indirect one is placed first.
  e.g. me lo da – he gives it to me.

If both pronouns are in the third person, **se** is used as indirect object.
  e.g. se lo da – he gives it to him.

When speaking to strangers always use the forms **usted** and **ustedes**.
Tú and **vosotros** are used to close friends and to children.

DEMONSTRATIVE PRONOUNS

this one, that one

	m	*f*
this (one)	éste	ésta
these	éstos	éstas
that (one)	ése	ésa
those	ésos	ésas
that (one) over there	aquél	aquélla
those	aquéllos	aquéllas

They agree in number and gender with the nouns they represent.
e.g. éste es mi bolígrafo – this is my ball-point.

quiero esta postal, ésa, y aquélla – I want this postcard, that one, and that one over there.

The demonstrative adjectives have the same form as the pronouns, except that they are not written with accents.

VERBS

'To be' is translated by **ser** and **estar**.

When it is followed by a noun, or when it indicates an origin, or a permanent or inherent quality, **ser** is used.

e.g. la nieve es fría y blanca   snow is cold and white
soy inglés   I am English
Inglaterra es una isla   England is an island

When it indicates position or a temporary state, **estar** is used.

    e.g. el hotel está en la calle principal   the hotel is in the main street
         estamos en España   we are in Spain

Present tense of **ser** and **estar**

	ser	*estar*
I am	soy	estoy
you are	eres	estás
he, she is,	es	está
you are	es	está
we are	somos	estamos
you are	sois	estáis
they, you are	son	están

'To have, to possess' is translated by **tener**.

I have, etc.	tengo
	tienes
	tiene
	tenemos
	tenéis
	tienen

    e.g. tengo mi pasaporte – I have my passport.

'To have' = **haber** is only used to form compound tenses of other verbs.

    e.g. he visto el hotel – I've seen the hotel.

I have, etc.	he
	has
	ha
	hemos
	habéis
	han

In Spanish there are three types of verbs, distinguished by the endings of the infinitives.

    -ar   hablar – to speak
    -er   vender – to sell
    -ir   vivir – to live

The present tense is formed as follows:

hablar	*vender*	*vivir*
hablo	vendo	vivo
hablas	vendes	vives
habla	vende	vive
hablamos	vendemos	vivimos
habláis	vendéis	vivís
hablan	venden	viven

The present tense of some common irregular verbs:

dar, to give	*decir*, to say	*hacer*, to do, make
doy	digo	hago
das	dices	haces
da	dice	hace
damos	decimos	hacemos
dais	decís	hacéis
dan	dicen	hacen

ir, to go	*poder*, can, to be able	*poner*, to put
voy	puedo	pongo
vas	puedes	pones
va	puede	pone
vamos	podemos	ponemos
vais	podéis	ponéis
van	pueden	ponen

querer, to want, to love	*traer*, to bring	*venir*, to come
quiero	traigo	vengo
quieres	traes	vienes
quiere	trae	viene
queremos	traemos	venimos
queréis	traéis	venís
quieren	traen	vienen

The past participle is formed by dropping the infinitive ending and adding the following endings to the stem of the verb.

-ar	hablar – to speak	**-ado**	hablado – spoken
-er	vender – to sell	**-ido**	vendido – sold
-ir	vivir – to live	**-ido**	vivido – lived

Some common irregular past participles:

abierto from abrir – opened
dicho from decir – said
escrito from escribir – written
hecho from hacer – made, done
puesto from poner – put
visto from ver – seen

The imperfect tense

	hablar		*vender*
I was speaking,	hablaba	I was selling,	vendía
used to speak,	hablabas	used to sell,	vendías
spoke, etc.	hablaba	sold, etc.	vendía
	hablábamos		vendíamos
	hablabais		vendíais
	hablaban		vendían

Verbs ending in **-ir** (vivir) have the same endings in the imperfect as those in **-er** (vender).

Irregular imperfect tense of **ser** – to be

era
eras
era
éramos
erais
eran

The future is formed by adding the following endings to the infinitives of all regular verbs:

hablar	*vender*	*vivir*
hablaré	venderé	viviré
hablarás	venderás	vivirás
hablará	venderá	vivirá
hablaremos	venderemos	viviremos
hablaréis	venderéis	viviréis
hablarán	venderán	vivirán

The negative is formed by putting **no** before the verb.

    e.g. no hablo español – I don't speak Spanish.

Essentials

First things

Yes	Sí
No	No
Please	Por favor
Thank you	Gracias
You're welcome *(in reply to thanks)*	De nada
No thank you	No gracias
Sorry	Perdone

Language problems

I'm English/American	Soy inglés/americano (inglesa/ americana)
Do you speak English?	¿Habla inglés?
Does anyone here speak English?	¿Habla inglés alguien aquí?
I don't speak Spanish	No hablo español
Do you understand (me)?	¿(Me) entiende?
I don't understand	No entiendo
Would you say that again, please?	Repita eso, por favor
Please speak slowly	Hable despacio, por favor
What is it called in Spanish?	¿Cómo se dice en español?
What does that mean?	¿Qué significa eso?
Can you translate this for me?	¿Puede traducirme esto?
Please write it down	Por favor escríbamelo

Questions

Where is/are . . . ?	¿Dónde está/están . . . ?
When?	¿Cuándo?
Who?	¿Quién?
Why?	¿Por qué?

What?	¿Qué?
How?	¿Cómo?
How much is/are ...?	¿Cuánto es/son ...?
How far?	¿Qué distancia hay?
What's that?	¿Qué es eso?
What do you want?	¿Qué desea?
What must I do?	¿Qué debo hacer?
Have you ...?	¿Tiene ...?
Is/are there ...?	¿Hay ...?
Have you seen ...?	¿Ha visto ...?
I want/should like ...	Quiero ...
What is the matter?	¿Qué pasa?
Can you help me?	¿Puede ayudarme?
Can I help you?	*¿Puedo ayudarle?
Can you tell/give/show me?	¿Puede decirme/darme/enseñarme?

Useful statements

I (don't) like it	(No) me gusta
I'm not sure	No estoy seguro
I don't know	No sé
I didn't know	No sabía

I think so	Creo que sí
I'm hungry/thirsty	Tengo hambre/sed
I'm tired	Estoy cansado/a
I'm in a hurry	Tengo prisa
I'm ready	Estoy listo/a
Leave me alone	Por favor déjeme
Just a moment	*Un momento
This way, please	*Por aquí/sígame
Take a seat	*Siéntese
Come in!	*¡Adelante!
It's cheap/expensive	Es barato/caro
It's too much	Es demasiado
That's all	Es todo
You're right	Tiene razón
You're wrong	No tiene razón
Thank you for your help	Muchas gracias por su ayuda
It's beautiful	Es bonito/precioso

Greetings

Good morning/good day	Buenos días[1]
Good afternoon	Buenas tardes
Good evening/good night	Buenas noches
Good-bye	Adiós
Hello	¡Hola!/ ¿qué hay?/adiós[2]
How are you?	¿Cómo está (usted)?
Very well, thank you	Muy bien, gracias
See you soon	Hasta luego
Have a good journey	¡Buen viaje!
Good luck/all the best	¡Buena suerte!

Polite phrases

Sorry/excuse me	Perdone
That's all right	Está bien
Everything all right?	¿Todo bien?
Not at all/don't mention it	De nada
Don't worry	No se preocupe
It doesn't matter	No importa

1. *Buenos días* and *buenas tardes* are often abbreviated to *buenas*.
2. *Adiós* is used when passing an acquaintance in the street.

I beg your pardon?	¿Qué/ ¿cómo dice?
Am I disturbing you?	¿(Le) molesto?
I'm sorry to have troubled you	Siento haberle molestado
Good/that's fine	Bien/está muy bien

Opposites

before/after	antes/después	an-tes/des-**pwes**
early/late	temprano/tarde	tem-pra-no/tar-de
first/last	primero/último	pree-mair-oh/**ool-tee-mo**
now/then	ahora/entonces	a-or-a/en-ton-thes
far/near	lejos/cerca	le-hos/thair-ka
here/there	aquí/allí	a-**kee**/a-ye
in/out	en/fuera	en/fwair-a
inside/outside	adentro/fuera	a-den-tro/fwair-a
under/over	debajo/sobre	de-ba-ho/so-bre
big, large/small	grande/pequeño	gran-de/pe-ken-yo
deep/shallow	profundo/poco profundo	pro-foon-do/po-co pro-foon-do
empty/full	vacío/lleno	ba-**thee**-oh/llye-no
fat/thin	gordo/fino	gor-do/fee-no
heavy/light	pesado/ligero	pe-sa-doh/lee-hair-o

high/low	alto/bajo	al-to/ba-ho
long, tall/short	largo, alto/corto	lar-go, al-to/kor-to
narrow/wide	estrecho/ancho	es-tre-cho/an-cho
many/few	muchos/pocos	moo-chos/po-kos
more/less	más/menos	mas/me-nos
much/little	mucho/poco	moo-cho/po-ko
beautiful/ugly	bonito/feo	bo-nee-to/fay-oh
better/worse	mejor/peor	me-hor/pe-or
cheap/dear	barato/caro	ba-ra-to/ca-ro
clean/dirty	limpio/sucio	leem-pyo/soo-thyo
cold/hot, warm	frio/caliente	free-oh/ca-lee-en-te
easy/difficult	fácil/difícil	fa-theel/dee-fee-theel
fresh/stale	fresco/pasado	fres-co/pa-sa-doh
good/bad	bueno/malo	bwe-no/ma-lo
young/old	joven/viejo	ho-ben/bye-ho
new/old	nuevo/viejo	nwe-bo/bye-lo
right/wrong	correcto/incorrecto	ko-rek-toh/een-ko-rek-toh
free/taken	libre/ocupado	lee-bre/o-koo-pa-doh
open/closed, shut	abierto/cerrado	a-byer-toh/ther-ra-doh
quick/slow	rápido/lento	ra-pee-doh/len-toh
quiet/noisy	tranquilo/ruidoso	tran-kee-lo/rwee-do-so

Signs and public notices[1]

Abierto de . . . a . . .	Open from . . . to . . .
Agua potable	Drinking water
Ascensor	Lift/elevator
Banco	Bank
Caballeros	Gentlemen
Caja	Cash desk
Cerrado	Closed
Circulen por la derecha	Keep right
Comisaría	Police
Correos	Post office
Empujar	Push
Entrada	Entrance
Entrada gratuita/libre	Admission free
Guía	Guide
Hay habitaciones	Vacancies/rooms to let

1. See also MOTORING (p. 50).

(Hotel) completo	No vacancies
Información	Information
Intérprete	Interpreter
Lavabos	Lavatory
Libre	Vacant/free/unoccupied
Liquidación	Sale
Llamar	Knock/ring
No hay entradas/localidades	House full (*cinema, etc.*)
No pasar	No entry
No pisar por la hierba	Keep off the grass
No tocar	Do not touch
Ocupado	Engaged/occupied
Particular/privado	Private
Peatones	Pedestrians
Peligro	Danger
Precaución	Caution
Prohibido ... bajo multa de ...	Trespassers will be prosecuted
Prohibido el paso	No entry
Reservado	Reserved
Retretes	Lavatory
Saldo	Sale
Salida	Exit
Salida de emergencia	Emergency exit
Se alquila	To let/for hire

Se alquilan habitaciones/ apartamentos	Rooms/flats to let
Señoras	Ladies
Señores	Gentlemen
Se prohibe fumar	No smoking
Se ruega no . . .	You are requested not to . . .
Servicios	Lavatory
Se vende	For sale
Tirar	Pull

Abbreviations

a. de J.C.	antes de Jesucristo	B.C.
a/c	al cuidado de	care of
Avda.	avenida	avenue
C/	calle	street
cía.	compañía	company
c/c	cuenta corriente	current account
d. de J.C.	después de Jesucristo	A.D.
EE UU	Estados Unidos	U.S.A.
d., dra.	derecha	right
h	hora	hour
f.c.	ferrocarril	railway

izq.	izquierda	left
Na. Sra.	Nuestra Señora	Our Lady
Nº, núm.	número	number
p. ej.	por ejemplo	for example
pág.	página	page
pta.	peseta	peseta
P.V.P.	precio venta al público	sale price to the public
R.E.N.F.E.	Red nacional de ferrocarriles españoles	Spanish railways
S., Sta.	san, santa	saint
S. A.	sociedad anónima	ltd, inc.
Sr.	señor	Mr
Sra.	señora	Mrs
Srta.	señorita	Miss
V, Ud.	usted	you

Money[1]

Is there an exchange bureau near here?	¿Hay algún banco cerca donde se pueda cambiar dinero?
Do you cash traveller's cheques?	¿Cambian cheques de viajero?
Where can I cash traveller's cheques?	¿Dónde puedo cambiar cheques de viajero?
I want to change some English/ American money	Quiero cambiar dinero inglés/ americano
How much do I get for a pound/ dollar?	¿A cuánto está la libra/el dólar?
What is the current rate of exchange?	¿A cuánto está el cambio?
Can you give me some small change?	Déme algo de dinero suelto, por favor
Will you take a personal cheque?	¿Aceptan cheques?
Do you have any identification?	*¿Tiene algo que le identifique?
Do you have a banker's card?	*¿Tiene una tarjeta de banco?

1. In Spain banks are open from 9 a.m. to 2 p.m. Monday to Saturday.

Sign here, please	*Firme aquí, por favor
Go to the cashier	*Vaya a la caja
Exchange	*Cambio

CURRENCY

Spanish currency is the peseta. A 5-peseta coin is commonly called a *duro*, and prices are sometimes quoted as so many *duros*, e.g. 20 *duros* means 100 pesetas.

Travel

On arrival

Passport control	*Control de pasaportes
Your passport, please	*El pasaporte, por favor
May I see your green card?	* ¿Me permite ver su tarjeta verde?
Are you together?	* ¿Viajan juntos?
I'm travelling alone	Viajo solo(a)
I'm travelling with my wife/ a friend	Viajo con mi esposa/un(a) amigo(a)
I'm here on business/on holiday	Vengo de negocios/de vacaciones
What is your address in Madrid?	* ¿(Cuál es) su dirección en Madrid?
How long are you staying here?	* ¿Cuánto tiempo va a estar usted aquí?
How much money have you got?	* ¿Cuánto dinero trae?
I have . . . pesetas/pounds/ dollars	Tengo . . . pesetas/libras/dólares

Customs	*Aduana
Goods to declare	*Artículos que declarar
Nothing to declare	*Nada que declarar
Which is your luggage?	*¿Cuál es su equipaje?
Do you have any more luggage?	*¿Tiene más equipaje?
This is (all) my luggage	Esto es (todo) mi equipaje
Have you anything to declare?	*¿Tiene algo que declarar?
I have only my personal things in it	Sólo llevo mis cosas personales
I have a carton of cigarettes and a bottle of brandy/wine	Llevo un cartón de tabaco y una botella de coñac/vino
Open your bag, please	*Abra la maleta, por favor
Can I shut my case now?	¿Puedo cerrar la maleta ya?
May I go through?	¿Puedo pasar ya?/ ¿puedo irme?
Where is the information bureau, please?	¿Dónde está (la oficina de) Información?
Porter	Mozo
Would you take these bags to a taxi/the bus?	Lléveme estas maletas a un taxi/al autobus
What's the price for each piece of luggage?	¿Cuánto cuesta cada bulto?
I shall take this myself	Yo llevo esto
That's not mine	Eso no es mío
How much do I owe you?	¿Cuánto le debo?

Signs to look for at stations, etc.

Arrivals	Llegadas
Booking office	Despacho de billetes/taquilla
Buses	Autobuses
Connections	Combinación
Departures	Salidas
Exchange	Cambio
Gentlemen	Servicios/caballeros/señores
Information	Información
Ladies	Servicios/señoras
Left luggage	Consigna
Lost property	Oficina de objetos perdidos
Luggage lockers	Consigna automática
No smoking	Se prohibe fumar
Refreshments[1]	Cafetería/fonda/bar/restaurante
Reservations	Reservas
Suburban lines	Trenes de cercanías/trenes cortos
Taxi rank	Parada de taxis
Tickets	Billetes
Underground	Metro
Waiting room	Sala de espera

1. In a station the *cafetería* serves drinks and snacks; the *fonda* also serves meals and lets rooms.

Buying a ticket[1]

Where is the nearest travel agency?	¿Dónde esta la agencia de viajes más próxima?
Tourist office	La oficina de turismo
Have you a timetable, please?	¿Tiene(n) un horario/una guía?
A ticket to ...	Un billete para ...
How much is it first class to ...?	¿Cuánto cuesta un billete de primera a ...?
A second class to ...	Un billete de segunda a ...
A single/one way to ...	Un billete de ida a ...
A return to ...	Un billete de ida y vuelta a ...
How long is this ticket valid?	¿Cuánto tiempo dura este billete?
A book of tickets, please[2]	Un taco (de billetes)
Is there a supplementary charge?	¿Hay que pagar algún suplemento?
Is there a special rate for children?	¿Hay un precio especial para niños?
How old is he/she?	*¿Qué edad tiene el niño?

1. *La RENFE*, the Spanish railway system, has an office in the centre of most large towns. As ticket offices at railway stations only issue tickets shortly before the departure of the train, most people book their tickets and reserve seats in advance at the *RENFE* office.

You can buy a ticket call a *kilométrico* if you intend to travel long distances in Spain. There is a substantial discount on the normal price. Inquire at the *RENFE* office.

2. This is only available for underground journeys.

By train and underground[1]

RESERVATIONS AND INQUIRIES

Where's the railway station (main station)?	¿Dónde está la estación de ferrocarril?
Where is the ticket office?	¿Dónde está la taquilla/ la oficina de billetes?
Two seats on the train tomorrow to . . .	Dos reservas para mañana en el tren para . . .
I want to reserve a sleeper	Quiero reservar una cama
How much does a couchette cost?	¿Cuánto cuesta una cama litera?
I want to register this luggage through to . . .	Quiero facturar este equipaje directamente a . . .
What sort of train is it?[2]	¿Qué clase de tren es?
Is there an earlier/later train?	¿Hay un tren antes/más tarde?
Is there a restaurant car on the train?	¿Lleva el tren restaurante?

CHANGING

Is there a through train to . . .?	¿Hay tren directo a . . .?
Do I have to change?	¿Hay que hacer transbordo?

1. For help in understanding the answers to these and similar questions see TIME (p. 143), NUMBERS (p. 149), DIRECTIONS (p. 48).
2. The following kinds of train run in Spain: *talgo*, *ter* and *electro tren* for which one pays first or second class fare plus a supplement; *rápido* and *expreso* – ordinary trains; *correo* and *autovía* are slow trains. *Autoexpreso* is the car–sleeper express.

Where do I change?	¿Dónde hay que transbordar?
When is there a connection to . . . ?	¿Cuándo hay combinación para ir a . . . ?

DEPARTURE

When does the train leave?	¿A qué hora sale el tren?
Which platform does the train to . . . leave from?	¿De qué andén sale el tren para . . . ?
Is this the train for . . . ?	¿Es éste el tren para . . . ?

ARRIVAL

When does it get to . . . ?	¿A qué hora llega a . . . ?
Does the train stop at . . . ?	¿Para el tren en . . . ?
How long do we stop here?	¿Cuánto tiempo paramos aquí?
Is the train late?	¿Tiene retraso el tren?
When does the train from . . . get in?	¿A qué hora llega el tren que viene de . . . ?
At which platform?	¿En qué andén?

ON THE TRAIN

We have reserved seats	Tenemos reservas
Is this seat free?	¿Está este asiento libre?
This seat is taken	Este asiento está ocupado
Conductor	Revisor

By air

Where's the airline office?	¿Dónde está la oficina de líneas aéreas?
I'd like to book two seats on the plane to ...	Quiero reservar dos billetes para el avión de ...
Is there a flight to ...?	¿Hay algún vuelo a ...?
Are there night flights to ...?	¿Hay vuelos nocturnos a ...?
When does it leave?	¿A qué hora sale el avión?
arrive?	¿A qué hora llega?
When's the next plane?	¿A qué hora es el próximo avión?
Is there a coach to the airport/town/centre?	¿Hay autobús al aeropuerto/ a la ciudad/al centro?
When must I check in?	¿A qué hora hay que presentarse?
Please cancel my reservation to ...	Quiero anular mi reserva para ...
I'd like to change my reservation to ...	Quiero cambiar mi reserva para ...
What is the flight number?	¿Cuál es el número de vuelo?

By boat

Is there a boat from here to . . .?	¿Hay barco de aquí a . . .?
How long does the boat take?	¿Cuánto tiempo tarda?
How often does the boat leave?	¿Cada cuánto tiempo sale el barco?
Does the boat call at . . .?	¿Toca (el barco) en . . .?
When does the next boat leave?	¿Cuándo sale el próximo barco?
Can I book a single berth cabin? a first-class/second-class/ luxury class cabin?	¿Puedo reservar un camarote individual?/un camarote de primera/de segunda/de lujo?
How many berths are there in this cabin?	¿Cuántas literas hay en esta cabina?
When must we go on board?	¿A qué hora hay que estar a bordo?
When do we dock?	¿A qué hora se desembarca?
How long do we stay in port?	¿Cúanto tiempo estamos en el puerto?
(Car) ferry	Ferry (de coches)

By bus or coach[1]

Where's the bus station/coach station?	¿Dónde está la estación de autobuses/coches de línea?
Bus stop	*Parada de autobuses
Request stop	*Parada discrecional
When does the coach leave?	¿A qué hora sale el coche?
When does the coach get to . . .?	¿A qué hora llega el coche a . . .?
What stops does it make?	¿En qué sitios para?
How long is the journey?	¿Cuánto se tarda?
We want to take a coach tour round the sights	Queremos visitar los sitios de interés en autocar
Is there a sightseeing tour?	¿Hay un recorrido turístico/ una excursión?
What is the fare?	¿Cuánto cuesta (el billete)?
Does the bus/coach stop at our hotel?	¿El autobús/el coche para en nuestro hotel?
Is there an excursion to . . . tomorrow?	¿Hay alguna excursión a . . . mañana?
Does this bus go to the town centre/beach/station?	¿Va este autobús al centro/a la playa/a la estación?
When's the next bus?	¿Cuándo sale el próximo autobús?

1. *La RENFE*, the railway company, also runs coaches between certain towns, and tickets can be bought from *RENFE* offices. Privately owned coaches, known as *coches de línea*, ply mainly between villages.

How often do the buses run?	¿Cada cuánto tiempo hay autobus?
Has the last bus gone?	¿Ha salido ya el último autobús?
Does this bus go near . . . ?	¿Pasa este áutobús cerca de . . . ?
Where can I get a bus to . . . ?	¿Dónde puedo tomar el autobús para . . . ?
Which bus goes to . . . ?	¿Qué autobús va a . . . ?
I want to go to . . .	Quiero ir a . . .
Where do I get off?	¿Dónde tengo que bajarme?
The bus to . . . stops over there	*El autobús de . . . para allí
You must take a number . . .	*Tome el . . .
You get off at the next stop	*Bájese en la próxima parada
The buses run every ten minutes/every hour	*Hay autobuses cada diez minutos/cada hora

By taxi

Please get me a taxi	Por favor, (llámeme) un taxi
Where can I find a taxi?	¿Dónde puedo encontrar un taxi?
Are you free?	¿Está libre?
Please take me to the Madrid hotel/the station/this address	Al hotel Madrid por favor/ a la estación/a esta dirección
Can you hurry, I'm late?	Dése prisa, por favor; llego tarde

Please wait for me here	Espere aquí, por favor
Stop here	Pare aquí
Is it far?	¿Está lejos?
How much do you charge by the hour/for the day?	¿Cuánto cobra por hora/todo el día?
How much will you charge to take me to . . .?	¿Cuánto costaría ir a . . .?
How much is it?	¿Cuánto es?
That's too much	Es demasiado

Directions

Excuse me – could you tell me . . . ?	¿Perdone, podría usted decirme . . . ?
Where is . . . ?	¿Dónde está . . . ?
How do I get to . . . ?	¿Por dónde se va a . . . ?
How far is it to . . . ?	¿Qué distancia hay a . . . ?
How many kilometres?	¿Cuántos kilómetros?
How do we get on to the motorway to . . . ?	¿Por dónde se sale a la autopista de . . . ?
Which is the best road to . . . ?	¿Cuál es la mejor carretera para . . . ?
Is there a scenic route to . . . ?	¿Hay una ruta pintoresca a . . . ?
Where does this road lead to?	¿A dónde va esta carretera?
Is it a good road?	¿Es buena la carretera?
Is there a motorway?	¿Hay autopista?
Will we get to . . . by evening?	¿Llegaremos a . . . antes de anochecer?
Where are we now?	¿Dónde estamos ahora?

What is the name of this place?	¿Cuál es el nombre de este sitio?
Please show me on the map	Indíquemelo en el mapa, por favor
It's that way	*Es por ahí
It isn't far	*No está lejos
Follow this road for 5 kilometres	*Siga esta carretera unos cinco kilómetros
Keep straight on	*Siga adelante/derecho
Turn right at the crossroads	*Tuerza a la derecha en el cruce
Take the second road on the left	*Tome la segunda carretera a la izquierda
Turn right at the traffic-lights	*Tuerza a la derecha en las luces de tráfico
Turn left after the bridge	*Tuerza a la izquierda después del puente
The best road is the ...	*La mejor carretera es la ...
Take the ... and ask again	*Tome la ... y pregunte de nuevo

Motoring

General

Where is the nearest garage?	¿Dónde está el garaje más proximó?
How far is the next petrol station?	¿A qué distancia está la próxima gasolinera?
Have you a road map?	¿Tiene un mapa de carreteras?
Where is there a car park?	¿Dónde hay un aparcamiento?
Can I park here?	¿Puedo aparcar aquí?
How long can I park here?	¿Por cuánto tiempo puedo aparcar aquí?
May I see your licence/ logbook, please?	* ¿Su permiso/la documentación del coche, por favor?
Is this your car?	* ¿Es este su coche?

Car hire

Where can I hire a car?

¿Dónde puedo alquilar un coche?

I want to hire a small/large car

Quiero alquilar un coche pequeño/grande

How much is it by the hour/day/week?

¿Cuánto cuesta por hora/por día/por semana?

Does that include mileage?

¿Está incluido el kilometraje?

The charge per kilometre is . . .

*El precio por kilómetro es . . .

Do you want full insurance?

* ¿Quiere seguro a todo riesgo?

May I see your driving licence?

* ¿Su permiso de conducir?

Can I return it to your office in . . .?

¿Puedo mandárselo a su oficina de . . .?

Could you show me how to work the lights/windscreen wipers/horn/this?

¿Enséñeme a usar las luces/el limpiaparabrisas/el claxon/esto?

Road signs

Aduana	Customs
Alto	Stop
Aparcamiento	Car park
Atención/Precaución	Caution

Autopista	Motorway
Calle estrecha	Narrow road
Carretera cortada	No through road
Carretera obstruida	Road blocked
Ceda el paso	Give way
Circulen por la derecha	Keep right
Cuidado/Precaución	Caution
Curvas (peligrosas)	(Dangerous) bends
Despacio	Slow
Desviación	Diversion
Dirección prohibida	No entry
Dirección única/obligatoria	One way street
Estacionamiento prohibido	No parking
Estacionamiento limitado	Limited parking
No adelantar	No overtaking
Obras	Road works
Paso a nivel	Railway (level) crossing
Peage	Toll
Peatones	Pedestrians
Peligro	Danger
Prohibido adelantar	No overtaking
Prohibido el paso	No entry
Salida de camiones	Lorry exit
Zona azul	Limited parking zone

At the garage or petrol station

... litres of standard/premium petrol please

... litros de normal/super, por favor

Please check the oil and water

Mire el aceite y el agua, por favor

Fill it up please

Llénelo, por favor

How much is petrol a litre?

¿Cuánto cuesta el litro de gasolina?/¿A cuánto el litro?

The oil needs changing

El aceite necesita cambiarse

Check the brakes/transmission fluid, please

Revíseme los frenos/la valvulina de la transmisión, por favor

Please clean the windscreen

Límpieme el parabrisas, por favor

Check the tyre pressure, please

Compruebe el aire, por favor

Please wash the car

Láveme el coche, por favor

Can I leave the car here?

¿Puedo dejar aquí el coche?

What time does the garage close?

¿A qué hora se cierra el garaje?

Where are the toilets?

¿Dónde están los servicios?

Repairs, etc.

Is there a . . . agent here?	¿Hay aquí agencia . . . ?
Have you a breakdown service?	¿Hay servicio de averías?
Is there a mechanic?	¿Hay un mecánico?
May I use your phone?	¿Puedo usar su teléfono?
My car's broken down, can you send someone to tow it?	He tenido avería en el coche, ¿puede mandarme una grúa?
Can you send someone to look at it?	¿Puede enviar a alguien que lo vea?
It is an automatic and cannot be towed	Es automático y no puede remolcarse
Where are you?	*¿Dónde está usted?
Where is your car?	*¿Dónde está su coche?
I am on the road from . . . to . . ., near kilometre post . . .	Estoy en la carretera de . . . a . . ., cerca del poste del kilómetro . . .
How long will you be?	¿Cuánto tiempo tardará?
I've lost my car key	He perdido la llave del coche
The battery is flat, it needs charging	La batería está desgastada, necesita cargarse
My car won't start	No arranca el coche
It's not running properly	No marcha bien
Please change the wheel	Cambie la rueda, por favor

This tyre is flat/punctured	Este neumático está desinflado/pinchado
The valve is leaking	La válvula pierde
The radiator is leaking	Gotea el radiador
The engine is overheating	El motor se calienta
The engine knocks/is firing badly	El motor detona/funciona mal
It's smoking	Está echando humo
Can you change this faulty plug?	¿Puede cambiarme esta bujía estropeada?
There's a petrol/oil leak	Pierde gasolina/aceite
There's a smell of petrol/rubber	Hay olor a gasolina/goma
There's a rattle	Hace ruido
Something is wrong with my car/the engine/the lights/the clutch/the gearbox/the brakes/the steering	Hay algo que no va bien en mi coche/el motor/las luces/el embrague/la caja de cambios/los frenos/la dirección
I've got electrical/mechanical trouble	Se me ha estropeado el coche: debe ser algo eléctrico/mecánico
The carburettor needs adjusting	El carburador precisa un reglaje
Can you repair it?	¿Pueden arreglarlo?
How long will it take to repair?	¿Cuánto tiempo necesita para arreglarlo?
What will it cost?	¿Cuánto costará?
When will the car be ready?	¿Cuándo estará el coche arreglado?

I need it as soon as possible/in three hours/in the morning	Lo necesito lo antes posible/ dentro de tres horas/mañana por la mañana
It will take two days	*Tardaremos dos días en arreglarlo
We can repair it temporarily	*Se puede arreglar provisionalmente
We haven't the right spares	*No tenemos los repuestos necesarios
We have to send for the spares	*Tenemos que pedir los repuestos
You will need a new ...	*Necesita un (una) ... nuevo (nueva)
Could I have an itemized bill, please?	¿Puede darme una factura detallada, por favor?

Parts of a car

accelerate	acelerar	a-the-le-rar
accelerator	el acelerador	a-the-le-ra-dor
anti-freeze	el anticongelante	anti-con-he-lan-te
axle	el eje	e-he
battery	la batería	ba-tai-ree-a
bonnet	el capó	ka-po
boot/trunk	el maletero	ma-le-ter-o

brake	el freno	fre-no
breakdown	la avería	a-ber-ee-a
bulb	la luz/bombilla	looth/bom-bee-llya
bumper	los parachoques	para-cho-kes
carburettor	el carburador	kar-boo-ra-dor
choke	el aire	a-ee-re
clutch	el embrague	em-bra-ge
crank-shaft	el cigüeñal	thee-gwe-nyal
cylinder	el cilindro	thee-leen-dro
differential gear	el diferencial	dee-fer-en-thee-al
dip stick	el indicador de nivel de aceite	een-dee-ka-dor de nee-bel de a-thay-te
distilled water	el agua destilada	agwa des-tee-la-da
distributor	el distribuidor	dee-stree-boo-ee-dor
door	la puerta	pwair-ta
doorhandle	la manilla	ma-nee-llya
drive (to)	conducir	kon-doo-theer
driver	el conductor	kon-dook-tor
dynamo	la dínamo	dee-na-mo
engine	el motor	mo-tor
exhaust	el (tubo de) escape	es-ka-pe
fan	el ventilador	ben-tee-la-dor
fanbelt	la correa del ventilador	kor-re-a del ben-tee-la-dor

(oil) filter	el filtro (de aceite)	feel-tro
foglamp	el antiniebla	anti-nee-eb-la
fusebox	la caja de fusibles	ka-ha de foo-see-bles
gasket	la empaquetadura	em-pa-ke-ta-doo-ra
gear-box	la caja de cambios/de velocidades	ka-ha de kam-bee-os/ de be-lo-thee-da-des
gear-lever	la palanca de cambios	pa-lan-ka de kam-bee-os
gears	los cambios (de velocidad)	kam-bee-os
grease (to)	engrasar	en-gra-sar
handbrake	el freno de mano	fre-no de ma-no
heater	la calefacción	ka-le-fak-thee-on
horn	la bocina/el claxon	bo-thee-na/klak-son
ignition	el encendido	en-then-dee-do
ignition key	la llave del contacto	llya-be del kon-tak-to
indicator	el indicador	een-dee-ka-dor
jack	el gato	ga-toh
key	la llave	llya-be
lights – full beam/ dipped headlights/ side (parking)	los faros – luz larga/ corta/de posición	fa-ros – looth lar-ga/ kor-ta/de po-see-thyon
mirror	el espejo	es-pe-ho
number plate	la (placa de) matrícula	ma-tree-koo-la

nut	la tuerca	twer-ka
oil	el aceite	a-thay-te
petrol	la gasolina	ga-so-lee-na
petrol can	la lata de gasolina	la-ta de ga-so-lee-na
piston	el émbolo	em-bo-lo
plug	la bujía	boo-**hee**-a
points	las conesiones	ko-ne-see-o-nes
(oil/water) pump	la bomba (de aceite/agua)	bom-ba
propellor shaft	el árbol de transmisión	ar-bol de trans-mee-syon
puncture	el pinchazo	peen-cha-tho
radiator	el radiador	ra-dee-a-dor
reverse	la marcha atrás	mar-cha at-**ras**
(sliding) roof	el techo (descapotable)	te-cho
seat	el asiento	a-see-en-toh
shock absorber	el amortiguador	a-mor-tee-gwa-dor
silencer	el silenciador	see-len-thee-a-dor
spanner	la llave inglesa	llya-be een-gle-sa
spares	los repuestos	re-pwes-tos
spare wheel	la rueda de repuesto	rwe-da de re-pwes-toh
speedometer	el cuentakilómetros	kwen-ta-kee-lo-me-tros
spring	el resorte/el muelle	re-sor-te/mwe-llye

stall (to)	atascarse	a-tas-kar-se
steering	la dirección	dee-rek-thyon
steering wheel	el volante	bo-lan-te
suspension	la suspensión	soos-pen-syon
tank	el depósito	de-po-see-toh
tappets	los alza-válvulas	al-tha-bal-boo-las
transmission	la transmisión	trans-mee-syon
tyre	el neumático	ne-oo-ma-tee-ko
valve	la válvula	bal-boo-la
wheel	la rueda	rwe-da
window	la ventanilla	ben-tan-ee-llya
windscreen	el parabrisas	pa-ra-bree-sas
windscreen washers	los lavaparabrisas	la-ba-pa-ra-bree-sas
windscreen wipers	los limpiaparabrisas	leem-pee-a-pa-ra-bree-sas

Accommodation[1]

Booking a room

Rooms to let/vacancies	*Hay habitaciones/se alquilan habitaciones/camas
No vacancies	*(Hotel) completo
Where is there a cheap hotel?	¿Dónde hay un hotel barato?
Have you a room for the night?	¿Tienen habitación para esta noche?
How long will you be staying?	*¿Cuánto tiempo van a estar?
Is it for one night only?	*¿Sólo una noche?
Do you know another good hotel?	¿Puede recomendarme otro hotel bueno?
I've reserved a room; my name is . . .	Tengo habitación reservada; mi nombre es . . .

1. See also LAUNDRY (p. 108) and RESTAURANT (p. 72).
In addition to privately owned hotels and pensions Spain also has state-run accommodation called *paradores, refugios* and *albergues de carretera*. You are not allowed to stay in an *albergue* for more than 48 hours.

I want a single room with a shower	Quiero habitación individual con ducha
We want a room with a double bed and a bathroom	Queremos habitación con cama de matrimonio y baño
Have you a room with twin beds?	¿Tienen habitación de dos camas?
I want a room with a washbasin	Quiero habitación con lavabo
Is there hot and cold water?	¿Hay agua caliente y fría?
I want a room for two or three days/a week/until Friday	Quiero habitación para dos o tres días/una semana/hasta el viernes
What floor is the room on?	¿En qué piso está la habitación?
Is there a lift/elevator?	¿Hay ascensor?
Have you a room on the first floor?	¿Tienen habitación en el primer piso?
May I see the room?	¿Puedo ver la habitación?
I'll take this room	Tomo esta habitación
I don't like this room	No me gusta esta habitación
Have you another one?	¿Tienen otra?
I want a quiet room	Quiero una habitación tranquila
There's too much noise in this room	Hay mucho ruido en esta habitación
I'd like a room with a balcony	Me gustaría una habitación con balcón
Have you a room looking on to the street/the sea?	¿Tienen habitación que dé a la calle/al mar?

Is there a telephone/radio/television/piped music in the room?	¿Hay teléfono/radio/televisión/hilo musical en la habitación?
We've only a twin-bedded room	*Sólo tenemos habitación doble
This is the only room vacant	*Esta es la única habitación que tenemos
We shall have another room tomorrow	*Tendremos otra habitación mañana
The room is only available tonight	*La habitación sólo está disponible esta noche
How much is the room per day?	¿Cuánto cuesta la habitación por día?
Have you nothing cheaper?	¿No tienen habitaciones más baratas?
What do we pay for the child/children?	¿Cuánto se paga por el niño/los niños?
Could you put a cot in the room?	¿Pueden poner una cuna/una camita en la habitación?
Is the service (and tax) included?	¿Está todo incluído?
Are meals included?	¿Están las comidas incluídas?
How much is the room without meals?	¿Cuánto es sólo la habitación?
How much is full board/half board?	¿Cuánto es la pensión completa/media pensión?
Do you do bed and breakfast?	¿Se puede tener habitación y desayuno?

Please fill in the registration form

* ¿Pueden llenar la hoja de registro, por favor?

Could I have your passport, please?

*El pasaporte, por favor

In your room

Room service

Servicio de piso

I'd like breakfast in my room, please

Quiero el desayuno en mi habitación

There's no ashtray in my room

No hay cenicero en mi habitación

Can I have more hangers, please?

Quisiera más perchas, por favor

Is there a point for an electric razor?

¿Hay enchufe para máquina de afeitar?

What's the voltage?[1]

¿Qué voltaje hay aquí?

Where is the bathroom?

¿Dónde está el baño?

Where is the lavatory?

¿Dónde están los servicios?

Is there a shower?

¿Tienen ducha?

There are no towels in my room

No hay toallas en mi habitación

There's no soap

No hay jabón

There's no (hot) water

No hay agua (caliente)

1. The most usual type of current in Spain is 127 volts and 50 cycles.

There's no plug in my washbasin	El lavabo no tiene tapón
The washbasin is blocked	El lavabo no corre
There's no toilet paper in the lavatory	No hay papel higiénico en el cuarto de baño
The lavatory won't flush	La cadena del cuarto de baño no funciona
May I have another blanket/another pillow, please?	Quisiera otra manta/otra almohada, por favor
The sheets on my bed haven't been changed	No han cambiado las sábanas de mi cama
I can't open my window; please open it	No puedo abrir la ventana; haga el favor de abrirla
It's too hot/cold	Hace demasiado calor/frío
Can the heating be turned up/down?	¿Pueden abrir/cerrar un poco más la calefacción?
Can the heating be turned on/off?	¿Pueden abrir/cerrar la calefacción?
Is the room air-conditioned?	¿Tiene la habitación aire acondicionado?
The air conditioning doesn't work	El aire acondicionado no funciona
Come in	Adelante/pase
Put it on the table, please	Póngalo en la mesa
I want these shoes cleaned	¿Pueden limpiarme los zapatos?
Could you get this dress/suit cleaned up a bit?	¿Pueden limpiarme un poco este vestido/traje?

I want this suit pressed	¿Pueden plancharme este traje?
When will it be ready?	¿Cuándo estará?
It will be ready tomorrow	*Estará listo mañana

At the porter's desk

My key, please	La llave (de mi cuarto), por favor
Please wake me at 8.30	Llámeme a las ocho y media
Are there any letters for me?	¿Tengo (alguna) carta?
Are there any messages for me?	¿Tengo algún recado?
If anyone phones, tell them I'll be back at 4.30	Si alguien llama por teléfono, digan que vuelvo a las cuatro y media
No one telephoned	*No ha telefoneado nadie
There's a lady/gentleman to see you	*Hay una señora/un señor preguntando por usted
Please ask her/him to come up	Que suba a mi habitación, por favor
I'm coming down (at once)	Bajo (en seguida)
Have you any writing paper/ envelopes/stamps?	¿Tienen papel de escribir/ sobres/sellos?
Please send the chambermaid	La camarera, por favor
I need a guide/interpreter	Necesito un guía/un intérprete

Can I leave this in your safe?	¿Puedo dejar esto en la caja fuerte?
Where is the dining room?	¿Dónde está el comedor?
What time is breakfast/lunch/ dinner?	¿A qué hora es el desayuno/la comida/la cena?
Is there a garage?	¿Hay aquí garaje?
Is the hotel open all night?	¿Está el hotel abierto toda la noche?
What time does it close?	¿A qué hora cierra?

Departure

I am leaving tomorrow	Me voy mañana
Can we check out at . . .?	¿Podemos liquidar a las . . .?
Can you have my bill ready?	¿Quiere darme la cuenta, por favor?
I shall be coming back on . . . can I book a room for that date?	Volveré el . . . ¿pueden reservarme habitación para ese día?
Could you have my luggage brought down?	¿Pueden bajarme el equipaje?
Please order a taxi for me at 11 a.m.	Quiero un taxi para las once
Thank you for a pleasant stay	Muchas gracias por todo

Meeting people

How are you/things?	¿Cómo está(n)?
Fine, thanks, and you?	Muy bien, gracias ¿y usted?
What is your name?	¿Cómo se llama?
My name is . . .	Soy . . ./Me llamo . . .
This is . . .	Este señor/esta señora es . . .
Have you met . . . ?	¿Conoce usted a . . . ?
Glad to meet you	Encantado
What lovely/awful weather	Qué estupendo/horrible tiempo
Isn't it cold/hot today?	Qué frío/calor hace hoy
Do you think it is going to rain/ snow?	¿Cree que va a llover/nevar?
Will it be sunny tomorrow?	¿Hará sol mañana?
Am I disturbing you?	¿Le molesto?
Go away	Márchese
Leave me alone	Déjeme en paz
Sorry to have troubled you	Siento molestar

Do you live/are you staying here?	¿Vive/está usted aquí?
Is this your first time here?	¿Es la primera vez que está aquí?
Do you like it here?	¿Le gusta esto?
Are you on your own?	¿Está solo(a)?
I am with my family/parents/a friend	Estoy con mi familia/mis padres/un amigo(a)
Where do you come from?	¿De dónde es usted?
I come from . . .	Soy de . . .
What do you do?	¿Qué hace usted?
What are you studying?	¿Qué estudia?
I'm on holiday/a business trip	Estoy de vacaciones/de negocios
Would you like a cigarette?	¿Quiere un pitillo?
Try one of mine	Tome uno de estos
They are very mild/rather strong	Son muy suaves/más bien fuertes
Do you have a light, please?	¿Tiene fuego, por favor?
Do you smoke?	¿Fuma?
No, I don't, thanks	No gracias
Help yourself	Sírvese
Can I get you a drink/another drink?	¿Puedo ofrecerle algo de beber/ otra copa?
I'd like a . . . please	Quisiera un . . . por favor
No thanks, I'm all right	No, gracias, estoy bien

Going out[1]

Are you waiting for someone?	¿Esperas a alguien?
Are you doing anything tonight/ tomorrow afternoon?	¿Tienes plan esta noche/ mañana por la tarde?
Could we have coffee/a drink somewhere?	¿Podemos tomar café/una copa (unos vinos)[2] en algún sitio?
Would you like to go out with me?	¿Quieres salir conmigo?
Shall we go to the cinema/theatre/ beach?	¿Vamos al cine/al teatro/a la playa?
Would you like to go dancing/ for a drive?	¿Quieres que vayamos a bailar/ a dar un paseo en coche?
Do you know a good disco/ restaurant?	¿Sabes cual es una buena discoteca/un buen restaurante?
Can you come to dinner/for a drink?	¿Puedes venir a cenar/a tomar una copa (unos vinos)[2]?
We are giving a party/there is a party; would you like to come?	Damos/hay una fiesta (un guateque)[3]; ¿quieres venir?
Can I bring a (girl) friend?	¿Puedo ir con un amigo (una amiga)?
Thanks for the invitation	Gracias por la invitación

1. Elsewhere in the book the polite form for 'you' has been used. Since this section deals with close personal relationships we have used the familiar form *tu*.
2. *Una copa* is quite formal; *unos vinos* is more commonly used by young people.
3. *Una fiesta* is a formal party; *un guateque* an informal party.

Where shall we meet?	¿Dónde nos encontramos?
What time shall I/we come?	¿A qué hora vengo/venimos?
I could pick you up at (*place*/*time*)	Puedo recogerte en . . . a las . . .
Could you meet me at (*time*) outside (*place*)?	¿Puedes recogerme a las . . . a la puerta de . . .?
What time do you have to be back?	¿A qué hora tienes que volver?
May I see you home?	¿Puedo acompañarte?
Can we give you a lift home/ to your hotel?	¿Podemos llevarte en el coche a tu casa/a tu hotel?
Can I see you again?	¿Puedo verte de nuevo?
Where do you live?	¿Dónde vives?
What is your telephone number?	¿Cuál es tu teléfono?
Do you live alone?	¿Vives solo (sola)?
Thanks for the drink/ride	Gracias por la copa/el paseo
It was lovely	Ha sido muy agradable
It was nice talking to you	Ha sido muy agradable charlar contigo
Hope to see you again soon	Espero verte pronto
See you soon/tomorrow	Hasta luego/hasta mañana

Restaurant

Going to a restaurant

Can you suggest a good/ cheap/vegetarian restaurant?	¿Puede recomendarnos un buen restaurante/un restaurante económico/ vegetariano?
I'd like to book a table for four at 1 p.m.	Quisiera reservar mesa para cuatro para la una
I've reserved a table; my name is . . .	Tengo mesa reservada a nombre de . . .
Have you reserved a table?	¿Han reservado una mesa?
We did not make a reservation	No hemos reservado
Have you a table for three?	¿Hay una mesa para tres?
Is there a table on the terrace/ by the window/ in a corner?	¿Hay mesa en la terraza/junto al ventanal/en un rincón?
This way, please	*Por aquí, por favor
We shall have a table free in half an hour	*Habrá mesa dentro de media hora

You will have to wait about .. minutes	*Tendrán que esperar unos ... minutos
We don't serve lunch until 1 p.m.[1]	*La comida no empieza hasta la una
We don't serve dinner until 9 p.m.	*No se sirven cenas hasta las nueve
We stop serving at 4 o'clock	*Dejamos de servir a las cuatro
Where is the lavatory?	¿Dónde están los servicios?
It is downstairs	*Están abajo
We are in a (great) hurry	Tenemos (mucha) prisa
Do you serve snacks?[2]	¿Sirven platos combinados/ bocadillos/pinchos?
That was a good meal, thank you	La comida estaba muy bien, gracias

Ordering

Waiter/waitress	Camarero/camarera
Service (not) included	Servicio (no) incluído
May I see the menu, please?	El menú/la carta, por favor

1. In Spain lunch is usually served from 1 p.m. to 4 p.m.; dinner from 8 p.m. to 11 p.m. Bars and cafés usually stay open until about 2 a.m.

2. A *plato combinado* is a main dish served in bars and cafés. It consists of various types of meat, vegetables, fish, eggs, etc., in different combinations. *Bocadillos* are more substantial than English sandwiches, consisting of half a Vienna loaf filled with meat, omelette, etc. *Pinchos* are quite substantial side dishes or hors d'œuvres which can make a meal in themselves.

May I see the wine list, please?	La lista de vinos, por favor
Is there a set menu?[1]	¿Tienen menú del día/menú turístico?
I want something light	Quiero algo ligero
Do you have children's helpings?	¿Hay media ración/reducción para niños?
What is your dish of the day?	¿Cuál es el plato del día?
What do you recommend?	¿Qué recomienda?
Can you tell me what this is?	¿Por favor, qué es ésto?
What is the speciality of the restaurant?	¿Cuál es la especialidad de la casa?
What is the speciality of the region?	¿Cuál es el plato típico de la región?
Would you like to try ...?	*¿Quiere probar ...?
There's no more ...	*No quedan ...
I'd like ...	Quiero ...
Is it hot or cold?	¿Es este plato caliente o frío?
Where are our drinks?	¿Dónde están nuestras bebidas?
Why is the food taking so long?	¿Por qué tardan tanto en servir la comida?
This isn't what I ordered, I want ...	Esto no es lo que he pedido, quiero ...
Without oil/sauce, please	Sin aceite/sin salsa, por favor

1. The *cubierto* is the all-in price of a meal, including wine, bread and sweet. Service is always included, though it is customary to leave a small tip. There is no cover charge in Spanish restaurants.

Some more bread, please	Más pan, por favor
Could we have some salt, please?	Queremos sal, por favor
A little more ...	Un poco más ...
This is bad	No está bueno
This is stale/tough	Está pasado/duro
This is too cold/salty	Esto está demasiado frío/salado
This plate/knife/spoon/glass is not clean	Este plato/cuchillo/cuchara/vaso no está limpio
This is undercooked/overcooked	Esto está poco hecho/demasiado hecho

Paying

The bill, please	La cuenta, por favor
Please check the bill – I don't think it's correct	Revise la cuenta, por favor, creo que no está bien
What is this amount for?	¿De qué es está cantidad?
I didn't have soup	No he tomado sopa
I had chicken, not lamb	Tomé pollo y no cordero
May we have separate bills?	¿Puede darme la cuenta por separado?
Keep the change	Deje el cambio

Breakfast and tea

A large white coffee	Un café con leche doble
A black coffee, please	Un café solo, por favor
I would like tea with (cold) milk/lemon	Un té con leche (fría)/limón
May we have some sugar, please?	Azúcar, por favor
A roll and butter	Pan y mantequilla
Toast	Tostadas
More butter, please	Más mantequilla, por favor
Have you some jam?	¿Tienen mermelada?
I'd like a soft-boiled/hard-boiled egg	Un huevo pasado por agua/cocido
Bacon and egg, please	Beicon y huevo, por favor
What fruit juices have you?	¿Qué zumos de frutas tienen?
Orange/grapefruit/tomato juice	Zumo de naranja/pomelo/tomate
Drinking chocolate	Chocolate hecho
Doughnut	Churros
Honey	Miel
Cake	Pastel/tarta

Snacks and picnics[1]

Can I have a . . . sandwich, please?	Un sandwich . . . por favor
What are those things over there?	¿Qué es eso que hay ahí?
What are they made of?	¿De qué está hecho?
What is in them?	¿Qué tiene dentro?
I'll have one of those, please	Uno de esos, por favor
Biscuits	Galletas
Bread	Pan
Cheese	Queso
Chocolate bar	Chocolatina
Eggs – boiled	Huevos – cocidos
fried	fritos
scrambled	revueltos
Ice cream	Helado
Light meals	Platos ligeros/pinchos
Meatballs	Albóndigas
Omelette	Tortilla
Pasties filled with meat or fish	Empanadillas
Sandwich	Bocadillo/sandwich
Toasted sandwich	Bocadillo caliente

1. See footnote p. 73.

Drinks[1]

Bar	El bar
Café	El café
What will you have to drink?	* ¿Qué quieren beber?
A bottle of the local wine, please	Una botella de vino de la tierra
The wine list please	La lista de vinos por favor
Carafe/glass	La jarra (de vino)/el vaso
Bottle/half bottle	Una botella/media botella
Good quality wine	Vino de marca
Vintage wine	Vino de reserva
Three glasses of beer, please	Tres cervezas, por favor
Do you have draught beer?	¿Tienen cerveza de barril?
Two more beers	Dos cervezas más
Large/small beer	Cerveza grande/pequeña
I'd like another glass of water, please	Otro vaso de agua, por favor
Neat/on the rocks	Solo/con hielo
With soda water	Con soda
Mineral water (still/fizzy)	Agua mineral (sin gas/con gas)
Ice (cubes)	(Cubos de) hielo
Cheers!	¡Salud!
The same again, please	Lo mismo

1. For the names of beverages, see pp. 91-2.

Three black coffees and one with milk	Tres cafés solos y uno con leche	
Coffee with a dash of milk	Un cortado	
Tea with milk/lemon	Té con leche/limón	
May we have an ashtray?	Un cenicero, por favor	
Can I have a light, please?	Una cerilla, por favor	

Restaurant vocabulary

ashtray	el cenicero	then-ee-thair-oh
beer	la cerveza	thair-be-tha
bill	la cuenta	kwen-ta
bread	el pan	pan
butter	la mantequilla	man-te-kee-llya
cigar	el puro	poo-roh
cigarettes	los cigarrillos/pitillos	thee-ga-ree-llyos/ pee-tee-llyos
cloakroom	el guardarropa	gwar-dar-ropa
coffee	el café	ka-fay
course/dish	el plato	pla-toh
cup	la taza	ta-tha
fork	el tenedor	te-ne-dor
glass	el vaso	ba-so
headwaiter	el maître	metr

hungry (to be)	tener hambre	te-nair am-bre
jug of water	la jarra de agua	har-ra de agwa
knife	el cuchillo	koo-chee-llyo
lemon	el limón	lee-**mon**
matches	las cerillas	the-ree-llyas
mayonnaise	la mayonesa	ma-yo-ne-sa
menu	el menú	me-noo
mustard	la mostaza	mos-ta-tha
napkin	la servilleta	sair-bee-llye-ta
oil	el aceite	a-thay-te
pepper	la pimienta	pee-mee-en-ta
plate	el plato	pla-toh
restaurant	el restaurante	res-tow-ran-te
salt	la sal	sal
sauce	la salsa	sal-sa
saucer	el platillo	pla-tee-llyo
service	el servicio	sair-bee-thee-oh
spoon	la cuchara	koo-cha-ra
sugar	el azúcar	a-**thoo**-kar
table	la mesa	me-sa
tablecloth	el mantel	man-tel
thirsty (to be)	tener sed	te-nair se
tip	la propina	pro-pee-na
toothpick	el palillo	pal-ee-llyo

vegetarian	vegetariano	be-he-ta-rya-no
vinegar	el vinagre	bee-na-gray
waiter	el camarero	ka-ma-rair-oh
waitress	la camarera	ka-ma-rair-a
water	el agua	ag-wa

The menu

ENTREMESES	HORS D'ŒUVRES
Aceitunas	olives
Alcachofas	artichokes
Anchoas	anchovies
Arenques	herring
Boquerones/chanquetes	fresh anchovies
Caracoles	snails
Chorizo	spicy sausage
Ensalada	salad
Ensaladilla rusa	Russian salad
Entremeses variados	mixed hors d'œuvres
Espárragos	asparagus
Fiambres	cold cuts
Gambas	prawns

Gambas al ajillo	prawns with oil and garlic
Gambas a la plancha	grilled prawns
Huevos rellenos	stuffed eggs
Jamón serrano	smoked ham
Jamón de york	boiled ham
Melón	melon
Ostras	oysters
Percebes	goose barnacles
Quisquillas	shrimps
Sardinas	sardines

SOPAS	SOUPS
Caldo/consomé	consommé
Caldo de gallina	chicken consommé
Cocido madrileño	meat and vegetable soup/stew
Consomé al jerez	consommé with sherry
Gazpacho	cold soup of tomatoes, cucumber, olive oil, garlic, etc.
Sopa de ajo	garlic soup with bread, egg and meat
Sopa de cebolla	onion
Sopa de fideos	noodle
Sopa de gallina	chicken

Sopa de mariscos	shellfish
Sopa de pescado	fish
Sopa de verduras	vegetable

PESCADOS	FISH
Almejas	clams
Anguila	eel
Atún/bonito	fresh tunny
Bacalao	(dried) cod
Bacalao a la Vizcaína	cod stewed with olive oil, peppers, onion and tomatoes
Bacalao al Pil-Pil	cod stewed in olive oil to produce a thick, rich sauce
Besugo	sea bream
Calamares	squid
Calamares en su tinta	squid cooked in their own ink
Cangrejo (de mar)	crab
Cangrejo (de río)	crayfish
Centolla	spider crab
Chipirones	baby squid
Gambas	prawns
Langosta	lobster
Lenguado	sole
Mariscos	seafood
Mejillones	mussels

Merluza	hake
Mero	grouper
Ostra	oyster
Pescadillo frito	mixed fried fish
Pez espada	swordfish
Pulpo	octopus
Quisquillas	shrimps
Rape	monkfish
Raya	skate
Rodaballo	turbot
Salmón	salmon
Salmonete	red mullet
Sardinas a la plancha	sardines 'grilled' on the hot plate
Sardinas en escabeche	pickled sardines
Vieiras	scallops
Zarzuela	fish and sea food in a sauce of tomatoes, onions, garlic, bay leaves, olive oil and wine

CARNE	MEAT
Albóndigas	meatballs/rissoles in a tasty sauce
Butifarra con judías	pork sausage with beans
Cabrito	kid
Callos	tripe

Carnero	mutton
Cerdo	pork
Chorizo	sausage made from spiced, cured pig meat
Chuleta	chop
Cochinillo	sucking pig
Cordero asado	roast lamb
Embutidos	sausages
Escalope	escalope
Estofado	stew
Fabada	black pudding and bean stew
Filete	fillet/cutlet
Guisado de ternera	veal stew
Hígado	liver
Jamón	ham
Lacón con grelos	forehams with turnip tops
Lengua	tongue
Lechazo	baby lamb
Lomo	loin
Mollejas	sweetbreads
Morcilla	black pudding
Pote gallego	hotpot
Riñones (al jerez)	kidneys (with sherry)
Salchichas	sausages

Sesos (huecos)	brains (fried)
Solomillo de puerco	pork fillet
Ternera	veal
Tostón	sucking pig
Vaca	beef

AVES Y CAZA / POULTRY AND GAME

Carne de venado	venison
Conejo	rabbit
Faisán	pheasant
Ganso	goose
Liebre	hare
Pato	duck
Pavo	turkey
Pechuga	chicken breast
Perdiz	partridge
Pichones	pigeons
Pollo	chicken

ARROZ / RICE

Arroz catalana	rice with pork, spicy sausages and fish
Arroz marinera	rice with seafood

Pollo con arroz	rice with chicken
Paella valenciana	saffron rice with chicken and seafood

LEGUMBRES Y VERDURAS

VEGETABLES

Ajo	garlic
Alcachofa	artichoke
Alubias	beans
Apio	celery
Berenjena	aubergine/eggplant
Cebolla	onion
Champiñón	mushroom
Coles	Brussels sprouts
Coliflor	cauliflower
Escarola	endive
Espárragos	asparagus
Espinacas	spinach
Garbanzos	chickpeas
Guisantes	peas
Habas	broad beans
Judías	green beans
Lechuga	lettuce
Lentejas	lentils
Nabo	turnip

Patata	potato
Puerro	leek
Pepino	cucumber
Perejil	parsley
Pimiento	pepper
Rábano	radish
Remolacha	beetroot
Repollo	cabbage
Seta	mushroom
Tomate	tomato
Zanahoria	carrot

HUEVOS	EGGS
Cocidos/duros	hard-boiled
Escalfados	poached
Fritos	fried
Huevos a la flamenca	eggs baked with onion, tomato and ham
Pasados por agua	soft-boiled
Revueltos	scrambled
Tortilla francesa	plain omelette
Tortilla de champiñones	mushroom omelette
Tortilla de espárragos	asparagus omelette
Tortilla de habas	broad bean omelette
Tortilla de patatas	potato omelette

QUESO	CHEESE
Burgos	soft creamy cheese from Burgos
Cabrales	strong cheese made from ewe's milk
Mahón	fairly bland cheese from Menorca
Manchego	hard cheese made from ewe's milk in La Mancha
Roncal	sharp tasting smoked cheese made from ewe's milk in northern Spain

POSTRES	DESSERTS
Almendrado	macaroon
Buñuelos	fritters
Compota	compote
Flan	crème caramel
Granizado	water ice
Helado	ice cream
de café	coffee
de chocolate	chocolate
de fresa	strawberry
de vainilla	vanilla
Mantecado	enriched ice cream
Mazapán	marzipan
Melocotón en almíbar	peaches in syrup

Merengue	meringue
Natilla	Spanish custard
Pastel/tarta	cake
Tarta helada	ice cream cake
Turrón	kind of nougat
Yemas	candied egg yolks

FRUTAS Y NUECES — FRUIT AND NUTS

Albaricoque	apricot
Almendra	almond
Avellana	hazel nut
Cereza	cherry
Chirimoya	custard apple
Ciruela	plum
Dátiles	dates
Fresa	strawberry
Higo	fig
Limón	lemon
Manzana	apple
Melocotón	peach
Melón	melon
Membrillo	quince
Naranja	orange
Pasas	raisins

Pera	pear
Piña	pineapple
Plátano	banana
Pomelo	grapefruit
Sandía	water melon
Toronja	grapefruit
Uvas	grapes

BEBIDAS / DRINKS

Agua	water
Agua mineral	mineral water
Anís	anise
Cerveza	beer
Coñac	brandy
Gaseosa	fizzy drink
Ginebra	gin
Horchata	cold drink made from chufa root or almonds
Leche	milk
Limonada	lemonade
Naranjada	orangeade
Ron	rum

Sangría	red wine mixed with soda water (or champagne), served with ice cubes and slices of lemon and orange
Sidra	cider
Vino	wine
blanco	white
dulce	sweet
espumoso	sparkling
rosé	rosé
seco	dry
tinto	red
Zumo de frutas	fruit juices

SOME COOKING METHODS AND SAUCES

ahumado	smoked
a la parilla	grilled
a la plancha	'grilled' on the hot plate
asado	roast
a la brasa/a la barbacoa	barbecued
caliente/frío	hot/cold
carne	meat
poco hecha	rare
corriente	medium
muy hecha	well-done
cocido	boiled
cocido al vapor	steamed

crudo	raw
escalfado	poached
frito	fried
gratinado	grated
guisado/estofado	braised/stewed
horneado	baked
marinado	marinated
relleno	stuffed
al aspic	in aspic
a la catalana	with tomatoes and green peppers
a la vasca	with parsley, garlic and peas
con perejil	with parsley
con mantequilla/aceite	with butter/oil
en escabeche	marinated in a sweet and sour sauce
salsa allioli	oil and garlic sauce
salsa mahonesa	mayonnaise
salsa romesco	sauce of tomatoes, garlic and hot peppers
salsa vinagreta	vinaigrette

Shopping[1] and services

Where to go

Which is the best . . . ?	¿Cuál es el mejor . . . ?	
Can you recommend a . . . ?	¿Puede usted recomendarme . . . ?	
Where is the market?	¿Dónde está el mercado?	
Is there a market every day?	?Hay mercado todos los días?	
Where's the nearest chemist?	¿Dónde está la farmacia más próxima?	
Where can I buy . . . ?	¿Dónde puedo comprar . . . ?	
When are the shops open?	¿Cuándo abren las tiendas?	
antique shop	la tienda de antigüedades	tyen-da day an-tee-gwe-da-des
baker	la panadería	pa-na-dair-ee-a
barber (see p. 106)	la barbería	bar-bair-ee-a

1. Shops are open from 9 or 9.30 a.m. to 1.30 p.m., and from 3 or 4 p.m. to 7.30 p.m

bookshop	la librería	lee-brair-**ee**-a
butcher (see p. 84)	la carnicería	kar-nee-thair-**ee**-a
chemist (see. p. 100)	la farmacia	far-ma-thee-a
confectioner	la pastelería	pas-tel-air-**ee**-a
dairy	la lechería	le-chair-**ee**-a
delicatessen (see p. 81)	la mantequería	man-te-kair-**ee**-a
department store (see pp. 97 and 102)	los almacenes	alma-**then**-es
dry cleaner (see p. 108)	la tintorería	teen-tor-air-**ee**-a
fishmonger (see. p. 83)	la pescadería	pes-ka-dair-**ee**-a
florist	la florería	flor-air-**ee**-a
greengrocer (see. pp. 87 and 90)	la verdulería	bair-doo-lair-**ee**-a
grocer (see pp. 81 and 105)	(la tienda de) alimentación/ comestibles	(tyen-da day) a-lee-men-ta-**thyon**/ ko-mes-tee-bles
haberdashery	la mercería	mair-thair-**ee**-a
hairdresser (see p.106)	la peluquería	pe-loo-kair-**ee**-a
hardware shop (see p. 107)	la ferretería	fer-re-te-**ree**-a
jeweller	la joyería	hoy-air-**ee**-a
launderette/laundry (see p. 108)	la lavandería	la-ban-dair-**ee**-a
liquor/wine store	la tienda de licores/ vinos	tyen-da day lee-kor-es/ bee-nos

newsagent (see p. 109)	el quiosco de periódicos	kyos-ko day pee-**ryo**-dee-kos
optician	el óptico	**op**-tee-ko
shoe repairer	el zapatero	tha-pa-tair-oh
shoe shop (see p. 104)	la zapatería	tha-pa-tair-ee-a
stationer	la papelería	pa-pe-le-ree-a
supermarket	el supermercado	soo-per-mer-ka-doh
tobacconist (see p. 111)	el estanco	es-tan-ko
toy shop	la juguetería/tienda de juguetes	hoo-ge-tair-ee-a/tyen-da de hoo-ge-tes

In the shop

Self service	*Autoservicio
Sale (clearance)	*Saldo/liquidación
Cash desk	*Caja
Shop assistant	El dependiente
Manager	El encargado/el jefe
Can I help you?	*¿Qué desea?
I want to buy ...	Quiero comprar ...
Do you sell ...?	¿Venden ustedes ...?
I'm just looking round	Voy a dar una vuelta

I don't want to buy anything now	Por el momento no voy a comprar nada
Could you show me . . . ?	¿Puede enseñarme . . . ?
We do not have that	*No tenemos eso
You'll find them in the . . . department	*Eso lo encontrará en el departamento de . . .
We've sold out but we'll have more tomorrow	*No tenemos ahora pero tendremos mañana
Can I order one?	¿Puedo encargar uno?
Anything else?	* ¿Algo más?
That will be all	Esto es todo
Shall we send it, or will you take it with you?	* ¿Se lo mandamos, o lo lleva usted?
I will take it with me	Lo llevo
Please send them to . . .	Mándenlos a . . .

Choosing

I want something in leather/green	Quiero algo en piel/verde
I need it to match this	Quiero que combine con esto
I like the colour but not the style	Me gusta el color pero no el estilo
I want a darker/lighter shade	Quiero un tono más oscuro/ más claro
I need something warmer/thinner	Necesito algo más caliente/ más ligero

Do you have one in another colour/size?	¿Tiene otro color/talla?
Have you anything better/cheaper?	¿Tienen algo mejor/más barato?
That is too much	Es demasiado
What size is this?	¿Qué talla es esta?
Have you a larger/smaller one?	¿Tienen mayor/más pequeña?
I take size . . .[1]	Uso la talla . . .
The English/American size is . . .	La talla inglesa/americana es . . .
Can I try it on?	¿Puedo probármelo?
It's too short/long/tight/loose	Es demasiado corto/largo/estrecho/ancho
Could I see that one, please?	¿Puedo ver ese, por favor?
What is it made of?	¿De qué es?/¿de qué está hecho?
For how long is it guaranteed?	¿Por cuánto tiempo está garantizado?

Colours

beige	beige	bezh
black	negro	ne-gro
blue	azul	a-thool
brown	marrón	mar-ron
gold	oro	or-oh
green	verde	bair-deh

1. See p. 103.

grey	gris	grees
orange	naranja	na-ran-ha
pink	rosa	ro-sa
purple	morado	mo-ra-doh
red	rojo	ro-ho
silver	plata	pla-ta
white	blanco	blan-ko
yellow	amarillo	a-ma-ree-llyo

Complaints

I want to see the manager	Quiero hablar con el jefe
I bought this yesterday	Compré esto ayer
It doesn't work/fit	No funciona/sirve
This is dirty/stained/torn/broken/cracked/bad	Está sucio/manchado/roto/estropeado/rajado/en malas condiciones
Will you change it, please?	¿Pueden cambiármelo?
Will you refund my money?	¿Pueden devolverme el dinero?
The receipt	El recibo

Paying

How much is this?	¿Cuánto es esto?
That's 500 pesetas, please	*Son quinientas pesetas
They are 20 pesetas each	*Son veinte pesetas cada uno
How much does that come to?	¿Cuánto es?
That will be . . .	*Importará/serán . . .
Can I pay with English/American currency?	¿Puedo pagar con dinero ingles/americano?
Do you take credit-cards/traveller's cheques?	¿Aceptan tarjetas de crédito/cheques de viajero?
Do you give any discount?	¿Hacen descuento?
Please pay the cashier	*Pague en la caja
May I have a receipt, please	Quiero un recibo, por favor
You've given me the wrong change	Creo que el cambio no está bien

Chemist[1]

Can you prepare this prescription for me, please?	¿Pueden hacerme esta receta, por favor?
When will it be ready?	¿Cuándo estará listo?
Have you a small first-aid kit?	¿Tienen un pequeño botiquín de urgencia?

1. See also AT THE DOCTOR'S (p. 130).

I want some aspirin/sun cream (for children)	Aspirinas/crema para el sol (para niños)
Can you suggest something for indigestion/constipation/diarrhoea?	¿Puede recomendarme algo bueno para la indigestión/el estreñimiento/la colitis?
I want a mosquito repellant	Quiero algo contra los mosquitos
Can you give me something for sunburn?	¿Tienen algo para las quemaduras del sol?
I want some throat lozenges/stomach pills/ antiseptic cream	Pastillas para la garganta/el estómago/crema antiseptica
Do you have sanitary towels/cotton wool?	¿Tienen compresas higiénicas/algodón?
I need something for insect bites/travel sickness/a hangover	Algo para las picadas de insectos/el mareo/la resaca

Toilet requisites

A packet of razor blades, please	Un paquete de cuchillas de afeitar, por favor
How much is this after-shave lotion?	¿Cuánto cuesta esta loción para el afeitado?
A tube of toothpaste, please	Un tubo de pasta de dientes/un dentífrico, por favor
A box of paper handkerchiefs/a roll of toilet paper, please	Una caja de pañuelos de papel/un rollo de papel higiénico, por favor

I want some eau-de-cologne/ perfume/cream	Un frasco de colonia/ perfume/crema
May I try it?	¿Puedo probar?
A shampoo for dry/greasy hair, please	Champú para pelo seco/ grasiento, por favor
Do you have any suntan oil/cream?	¿Tienen aceite solar/crema solar?

Clothes and shoes[1]

I want a hat/sunhat	Quiero un sombrero/sombrero para el sol
I'd like a pair of gloves/shoes/ sandals	Quiero un par de guantes/ zapatos/sandalias
May I look at some dresses, please?	Quiero ver vestidos
I like the one in the window	Me gusta el del escaparate
May I try this?	¿Puedo probarme éste?
Where are beach clothes?	¿Dónde están los trajes de playa?
Where is the underwear/ haberdashery/coat department?	¿Dónde está la ropa interior/ la mercería/los abrigos?
Where can I find socks/stockings?	¿Dónde hay calcetines/medias?

1. For sizes see pp. 103 and 104.

I am looking for a blouse/bra/ trousers/jacket/sweater	Busco blusas/sujetadores/ pantalones/chaquetas/prendas de punto
I need a coat/raincoat/hat	Necesito un abrigo/un impermeable/un sombrero
Do you sell buttons/elastic/zips?	¿Venden botones/goma/ cremalleras?
I want a short-/long-sleeved shirt, collar size . . .	Quiero una camisa de manga corta/larga, medida de cuello . . .
I need a pair of walking shoes with small heels	Un par de zapatos cómodos de tacón plano
These heels are too high/too low	Este tacón es demasiado alto/ bajo

Clothing sizes

WOMEN'S DRESSES, ETC.

British	32	34	36	38	40	42	44
American	10	12	14	16	18	20	22
Continental	30	32	34	36	38	40	42

MEN'S SUITS

British and American	36	38	40	42	44	46
Continental	46	48	50	52	54	56

MEN'S SHIRTS

British and American	14	14½	15	15½	16	16½	17
Continental	36	37	38	39	41	42	43

STOCKINGS

British and American	8	8½	9	9½	10	10½	11
Continental	0	1	2	3	4	5	6

SOCKS

British and American	9½	10	10½	11	11½
Continental	38–39	39–40	40–41	41–42	42–43

SHOES

British	1	2	3	4	5	6		7	8	9	10	11	12
American	2½	3½	4½	5½	6½	7½	8½	9½	10½	11½	12½	13½
Continental	33	34–5	36	37	38	39–40	41	42	43	44	45	46

This table is only intended as a rough guide since sizes vary from manufacturer to manufacturer.

Food[1]

Give me a kilo/half a kilo of . . ., please	Un kilo/medio kilo de . . ., por favor
100 grammes of sweets/chocolates	Cien gramos de caramelos/bombones
A bottle/litre of milk/wine/beer	Una botella/un litro de leche/vino/cerveza
Is there anything back on the bottle?	¿Devuelven algo por la botella?
I want a jar/tin/packet of . . .	Quiero un tarro/una lata/un paquete de . . .
Do you sell frozen foods?	¿Venden alimentos congelados?
These pears are very hard/soft	Estas peras están muy duras/blandas
Is it fresh?	¿Está fresco?
Are they ripe?	¿Están maduros?
This is bad	Está malo
A loaf of bread, please[2]	Un pan, por favor
How much a kilo/a bottle?	¿Cuánto cuesta el kilo/la botella?

1. See also the various MENU sections (p. 81 ff.) and WEIGHTS AND MEASURES (p. 152).
2. Spanish bread: *un pan de kilo (medio kilo)* – a loaf weighing 1 kilo (½ kilo); *un pan de barra* – a French loaf; *bollos/panecillos* – rolls; *un pan de molde* – English loaf.

Hairdresser and barber

May I make an appointment for this morning/tomorrow afternoon?	¿Pueden darme hora para esta mañana/para mañana por la tarde?
What time?	¿A qué hora?
I want my hair cut/trimmed	Quiero cortarme el pelo/ cortarme las puntas
Not too short at the sides	No demasiado corto de los lados
I'll have it shorter at the back	Más corto por atrás
My hair is oily/dry	Tengo el pelo grasiento/seco
I want a shampoo	Quiero que me laven la cabeza
I want my hair washed and set	Quiero que me laven y peinen
Please set it without rollers/on large/small rollers	Sin rulos, por favor/con rulos grandes/pequeños, por favor
Please do not use any hairspray	No me ponga laca
I want a colour rinse	Quiero un reflejo
I'd like to see a colour chart	¿Puedo ver colores?
I want a darker/lighter shade	Quiero un tono más oscuro/ claro
The water is too cold	El agua está demasiado fría
The dryer is too hot	El secador calienta demasiado
Thank you, I like it very much	Está muy bien
I want a shave/manicure, please	¿Pueden afeitarme/hacerme la manicura, por favor?

Hardware

Where is the camping equipment?	¿Utensilios de camping, por favor?
Do you have a battery for this?	¿Tienen pilas para esto?
Where can I get butane gas/paraffin?	¿Dónde se puede adquirir butano/parafina?
I need a bottle opener/tin opener/corkscrew	Necesito un abre-botellas/abrelatas/sacacorchos
A small/large screwdriver	Un destornillador pequeño/grande
I'd like some candles/matches	Velas/cerillas, por favor
I want a torch/knife/pair of scissors	Quiero una linterna/un cuchillo/unas tijeras
Do you sell string/rope?	¿Venden cuerda/soga?
Where can I find washing up liquid/scouring powder?	¿Dónde puedo comprar líquido lavavajillas/polvos de fregar?
Do you have dishcloths/brushes?	¿Tienen paños de cocina/cepillos?
I need a groundsheet/bucket/frying pan	Necesito una tela impermeable/un cubo/una sartén

Laundry and dry cleaning

Where is the nearest laundry/ dry cleaner?	¿Dónde está la lavandería/la tintorería más próxima?
I want to have these things washed/cleaned	Quiero que me laven/limpien esto
Can you get this stain out?	¿Se quitará esta mancha?
It is coffee/wine/grease	*Es de café/vino/grasa
These stains won't come out	*Estas manchas no se quitan
It only needs to be pressed	Sólo necesita plancharse
This is torn; can you mend it?	Esto está roto ¿pueden cosérmelo?
Do you do invisible mending?	¿Hacen zurcidos invisibles?
There's a button missing	Me falta un botón
Will you sew on another one, please?	¿Pueden ponerme otro?
When will they be ready?	¿Cuándo estarán?
I need them by this evening/ tomorrow	Los necesito para esta noche/ para mañana
Call back at 5 o'clock	*Vuelva a las cinco
We can't do it before Thursday	*No podemos hacerlo antes del jueves
It will take three days	*Estará dentro de tres días

Newspapers, writing materials and records

Do you sell English/American newspapers?	¿Venden periódicos ingleses/americanos?
Can you get . . . newspaper/magazine for me?	¿Pueden proporcionarme el diario . . ./la revista . . .?
Where can I get the . . .?	¿Dónde puedo comprar . . .?
I want a map of the city/a road map	Quiero un mapa de la ciudad/de carreteras
Is there an entertainment/amusements guide?	¿Hay una cartelera?
Do you have any English books?	¿Tienen libros ingleses?
Have you any books by . . .?	¿Tienen algún libro de . . .?
I want some picture postcards/plain postcards	Quiero unas tarjetas postales de vistas/tarjetas postales de correos
Do you sell souvenirs/toys?	¿Venden objetos de recuerdo/alguna clase de juguetes?
Do you have any records of local music?	¿Tienen discos de música regional?
Can I listen to this record please?	¿Puedo escuchar este disco?
Are there any new records by . . .?	¿Hay algún disco nuevo de . . .?
ballpoint	el bolígrafo
crayon	el carboncillo
drawing pins	las chinchetas
envelope	el sobre

file	la carpeta
glue	la cola de pegar
ink	la tinta
label	la etiqueta
pencil	el lápiz
string	la cuerda
writing paper	el papel de cartas

Photography

I want to buy a camera	Quiero una máquina fotográfica
Have you a film for this camera?	Tienen carretes para esta máquina?
I want a (fast) colour film/black and white film	Una película (rápida) en color/en blanco y negro
Would you fit the film in the camera for me, please?	Haga el favor de ponerme el carrete en la máquina
Does the price include processing?	¿Está el revelado incluído?
I'd like this film developed and printed	Quiero revelado y copias de este carrete
Please enlarge this negative	Quiero una ampliación de este negativo
When will it be ready?	¿Cuándo estará?
Will it be done tomorrow?	¿Estará mañana?
Will it be ready by . . .?	¿Puede estar para . . .?

My camera's not working, can you check it/mend it?	Esta máquina no funciona; ¿pueden revisarla/¿pueden arreglármela?
The film is jammed	No pasa el carrete
There is something wrong with the shutter/light meter/film winder	Va mal el obturador/el fotómetro/el carrete

Tobacconist[1]

Do you stock English/American cigarettes?	¿Tienen cigarrillos ingleses/americanos?
Virginia/dark tobacco	Tabaco rubio/negro
What cigarettes/cigars have you?	¿Qué (marcas de) cigarrillos/puros tienen?
A packet of . . ., please	Un paquete de . . .
I want some filter-tip cigarettes/cigarettes without filter/menthol cigarettes	Un paquete de cigarrillos con filtro/sin filtro/mentolados
A box of matches, please	Una caja de cerillas/fósforos
I want to buy a lighter	Quiero comprar un encendedor/mechero
Do you sell (lighter) fuel/flints?	¿Tienen cargas de gas/piedras (para el encendedor)?

1. Tobacconists also sell postage stamps. *Estancos* are recognized by a sign bearing the Spanish national colours (red, yellow, red).

I want a gas refill	Quiero un recambio de gas
Do you sell cigarette papers?	¿Tienen papel de fumar?

Repairs

This is broken, can you mend it?	Esto está estropeado, ¿pueden repararlo?
Could you do it while I wait?	¿Pueden hacerlo ahora mismo?
When should I come back for it?	¿Cuándo puedo recogerlo?
I want these shoes soled with leather/heeled with rubber	Quiero que me pongan mediasuelas de cuero/tacones de goma
Can you put on new heels?	¿Pueden ponerse tacones nuevos?
Can you repair this watch?	¿Pueden arreglarme este reloj?
I have broken the glass/strap/spring	Se me ha roto el cristal/la correa/el muelle
I have broken my glasses/the frames/the sides	Se me han roto las gafas/la patilla/la montura
How much would a new one cost?	¿Cuánto costaría una nueva?
The fastener/clip/chain is broken	El cierre/el clip/la cadena se ha roto
The stone is loose	La piedra está suelta
It can't be repaired	*No tiene arreglo
You need a new one	*Necesita un nuevo/una nueva

Post Office

Where's the main post office?	¿Dónde está la oficina principal de correos?
Where's the nearest post office?	¿Dónde está la oficina de correos más próxima?
What time does the post office open/close?	¿A qué hora abren/cierran correos?
Where's the post box?	¿Dónde hay un buzón de correos?
Which window do I go to for stamps/telegrams/money orders?	¿Cuál es la ventanilla de los sellos/los telegramas/los giros?

Letters and telegrams[1]

How much is a postcard abroad/ to England?	¿Qué franqueo llevan las tarjetas postales para el extranjero/para Inglaterra?
What's the airmail to the U.S.A.?	¿Qué franqueo llevan las cartas por avión para los Estados Unidos?
How much is it to send a letter surface mail?	¿Qué franqueo llevan las cartas por correo ordinario?
It's inland	Es para España
Give me three . . . peseta stamps, please	Tres sellos de . . . pesetas
I want to send this letter express	Quiero mandar esta carta urgente
I want to register this letter	Quiero certificar esta carta
Where is the poste restante section?	¿Dónde está la lista de correos?
Are there any letters for me?	¿Hay alguna carta a nombre de . . .?
What is your name?	*¿(Cuál es) su nombre, por favor/¿cómo se llama usted?
Have you any means of identification?	*¿Tiene algo que le identifique?
I want to send a (reply paid) te'egram	Quiero mandar un telegrama (con respuesta pagada)
How much does it cost per word?	¿Cuánto cuesta por palabra?

---

1. You can buy stamps from a tobacconist's as well as from a post office.

Telephoning[1]

Where's the nearest phone box?	¿Dónde hay un teléfono público?
May I use your phone?	¿Puedo usar su teléfono?
Do you have a telephone directory for . . .?	¿Tienen una guía telefónica de . . .?
I want to make a phone call	Quiero hacer una llamada telefónica
Please get me . . .	Quiero una conferencia con el . . .
I want to telephone to England	Quiero poner una conferencia a Inglaterra
Could you give me the cost/time and charges afterwards?	¿Puede decirme después cuánto es?
I want to reverse the charges/call collect	Quiero una conferencia con cobro revertido
I was cut off, can you reconnect me?	Me han cortado, ¿puede volverme a poner?
I want extension . . .	Quiero extensión . . .
May I speak to Señor Alvarez?	El señor Alvarez, por favor
Who's speaking?	¿De parte de quién/quién habla?
Hold the line, please	*No se retire

1. There are two kinds of telephone box: *urbanas* (using single peseta coins) for local calls only and *interurbanas* (using 5-peseta coins) for long-distance calls. You can also telephone from most bars and cafés. There is no link between the *correos* and the *telefónica*, they are separate services, and post offices do not contain telephones.

We'll call you back	Le llamaremos
He's not here	*No está en casa/aquí
He's at ...	*Está ...
When will he be back?	¿Cuándo volverá?
Will you take a message?	¿Puedo dejarle un recado?
Tell him that Mr X phoned	Dígale que ha llamado el señor X
I'll ring again later	Llamaré más tarde
Please ask him to phone me	Dígale que me llame, por favor
What's your number?	* ¿Cuál es su número?
My number is ...	Mi número es ...
I can't hear you	No le oigo bien
The line is engaged	*Comunica
There's no reply	*No contestan
You have the wrong number	*Tiene el número confundido

Sightseeing[1]

What ought one to see here?	¿Qué hay que ver aquí?
Is there a sightseeing tour/boat ride?	¿Hay excursiones/paseos en barco?
What's this building?	¿Qué edificio es éste?
Where is the old part of the city?	¿Dónde está la parte antigua de la ciudad?
When was it built?	¿Cuándo fué construído?
Who built it?	¿Quién lo construyo?
What's the name of this church?	¿Cómo se llama esta iglesia?
Is there a Protestant church/synagogue?	¿Hay aquí iglesia protestante/sinagoga?
What time is mass at . . . church?	¿A qué hora hay misa en la iglesia de . . .?
What time is the service?[2]	¿A qué hora es el servicio/el culto?

1. See also BY BUS OR COACH (p. 45), DIRECTIONS (p. 48).
2. *Servicio* is a service in a Protestant church, *culto* in a Catholic church.

Is this the natural history museum?	¿Es éste el museo de historia natural?
When is the museum open?	¿A qué hora está abierto el museo?
Is it open on Sundays?	¿Está abierto los domingos?
The museum is closed on Mondays	*El museo está cerrado los lunes
Admission free	*Entrada gratuita
How much is it to go in?	¿Cuánto cuesta la entrada?
Are there reductions for children/students?	¿Hay precios reducidos para niños/estudiantes?
Are entry fees reduced on any special day?	¿Hay algún día entradas más baratas?
Have you a ticket?	*¿Tiene usted entrada?
Where do I get tickets?	¿Dónde se sacan las entradas?
Please leave your parcels in the cloakroom	*Dejen los paquetes en el guardarropa
It's over there	*Está por allí
Can I take pictures?	¿Puedo sacar fotografías?
Photographs are prohibited	*Se prohíbe hacer fotografías
Follow the guide	*Siga al guía
Does the guide speak English?	¿Habla el guía inglés?
We don't need a guide	No necesitamos guía
Where is the . . . collection/exhibition?	¿Dónde está la colección/exposición de . . .?
Where are the Goyas?	¿Dónde está la sala de Goya?

Where can I get a catalogue?	¿Dónde se compran catálogos?
Where can I get a plan/guide book of the city?	¿Donde puedo comprar un plano/una guía de la ciudad?
Where do we find antiques/souvenirs/a shopping centre/the market?	¿Dónde encontraríamos antigüedades/objetos de recuerdo/un centro comercial/el mercado?
Is this the way to the zoo?	¿Se va por aquí al parque zoológico?
Which bus goes to the castle?	¿Qué autobús va al castillo?
How do I get to the park?	¿Cómo se va al parque?
Can we walk there?	¿Se puede ir andando?

Entertainment

Is there an entertainment guide?	¿Hay guía de espectáculos?
What's on at the theatre/cinema?[1]	¿Qué hay en los teatros/cines?
Is there a concert?	¿Hay algún concierto?
I want two seats for tonight	Quiero dos entradas para esta noche
I want to book seats for Thursday	Quiero reservar entradas para el jueves
That performance is sold out	*No hay billetes para esta sesión
Are they good seats?	¿Son estas entradas buenas?
Where are these seats?	¿Dónde están estos asientos?
What time does the performance start?	¿A qué hora empieza la función?
What time does it end?	¿A qué hora termina?
What should one wear?	¿Cómo hay que ir vestido?

1. Usually there are two performances daily in theatres and some cinemas. The first (*tarde*) begins at 7.30 or 8 p.m., the second (*noche*) at 10.30 or 11 p.m. Theatres often have two performances on Sundays, starting at 4.30 p.m. In other cinemas the show goes on continuously, starting at about 4.30.

Is evening dress necessary?	¿Es necesario el traje de etiqueta?
Where is the cloakroom?	¿Dónde está el guardarropa?
This is your seat	*Este es su asiento
A programme, please	Un programa, por favor
Which is the best nightclub?	¿Cuál es la mejor sala de fiestas?
What time is the floorshow?	¿A qué hora es el espectáculo?
May I have this dance?	¿Quiere bailar?
Is there a jazz club here?	¿Hay alguna sala/algún club de jazz?
Do you have a discotheque here?	¿Tienen discoteca?
Can you recommend a good show?	¿Puede recomendarnos algún espectáculo bueno?

Sports and games

Where is the nearest tennis court/ golf course?	¿Dónde están las pistas de tenis/ de golf más próximas?
What is the charge per game/ hour/day?	¿Cuánto cobran por juego/hora/ día?
Where can we go swimming/ fishing?	¿Dónde podríamos ir a nadar/ pescar?
Can I hire a racket/clubs/fishing tackle?	¿Puedo alquilar raqueta/palos de golf/aparejos de pescar?
Do I need a permit?	¿Se necesita un permiso?
Where do I get a permit?	¿Dónde dan el permiso?
Is there a skating rink/ski slope?	¿Hay pista de patinar/esquiar?
Can I hire skates/skiing equipment?	¿Puedo alquilar patines/equipo de esquiar?
Are there ski lifts?	¿Hay telesquí?
Can I take lessons here?	¿Dan lecciones aquí?
Where is the stadium?	¿Dónde está el estadio?

Are there any seats left in the grandstand?	¿Hay entradas de tribuna?
How much are the cheapest seats?	¿Cúanto cuestan las entradas más baratas?
Are the seats in the sun/shade?	¿Están estos asientos al sol/a la sombra?
We want to go to a football match/the tennis tournament/ the bullfight	Queremos ir a un partido de football/al campeonato de tenis/a los toros
Who's playing?	¿Qué equipo juega?
Who's (bull) fighting?	¿Quién torea?
When does it start?	¿A qué hora empieza?
What is the score?	¿Cómo va el marcador?
Who's winning?	¿Quién gana?
Where's the race course?	¿Dónde está el hipódromo?
Which is the favourite?	¿Cuál es el favorito?
Who's the jockey?	¿Quién es el jinete?
100 pesetas to win on . . ./each way on . . .	Cien pesetas a ganador/a ganador y colocado
What are the odds?	¿A cómo van las apuestas?
Do you play cards?	¿Juega a las cartas?
Would you like a game of chess?	¿Quiere que juguemos al ajedrez?

THE BULLFIGHT[1]	LA CORRIDA
The bull-ring	la plaza de toros
Tickets[2] 　in the sun (*cheaper*) 　in the shade (*more expensive*)	entradas 　de sol 　de sombra
Ringside (*best*) seats	barreras
Second-best seats	contrabarreras
Seats directly behind the 　*contrabarreras*	tendidos
A box	un palco
The gods	la galería
The balcony	el balconcillo
The bullfighter	el torero
Horsemen with lances who 　weaken the bull	los picadores
The men who place the darts in 　the bull's shoulder muscles	los banderilleros
The darts	las banderillas
Red and yellow cloak used at 　the beginning of the *corrida*	la capa/el capote
Small cape used for dangerous 　passes and preparation for the 　kill	la muleta
The kill	la estocada

1. *La novillada* is a corrida with young bulls and inexperienced bullfighters (*novilleros*).
2. For a good bullfight tickets cost from 700–2,000 pesetas.

The stabbing at the base of the skull if the bull is not killed immediately	el descabello
The ear (the bullfighter may be awarded one or both ears or the tail, depending on his performance)	la oreja
The tail	el rabo

On the beach

Which is the best beach?	¿Cuál es la mejor playa?
Is there a quiet beach near here?	¿Hay por aquí alguna playa tranquila?
Is it far to walk?	¿Se puede ir andando?
Is there a bus to the beach?	¿Hay autobús a la playa?
Is the beach sand/pebbles/rocks?	¿Es la playa de arena/piedras/rocas?
Is the bathing dangerous from this beach/bay?	¿Es peligroso bañarse en esta playa/bahía?
Is it safe for small children?	¿No es peligrosa para niños pequeños?
Does it get very rough?	¿Se pone el mar bravo?
Bathing prohibited	*Prohibido bañarse
It's dangerous	*Hay peligro
Is the tide rising/falling?	¿Está la marea subiendo/bajando?
There's a strong current here	*Aquí hay mucha corriente

You will be out of your depth	*No se hace pie
Are you a strong swimmer?	* ¿Nada bien?
Is it deep?	¿Hay mucha profundidad?
Is the water cold?	¿Está el agua fría?
It's warm	Está caliente
Can one swim in the lake/river?	¿Se puede nadar en el lago/río?
Is there an indoor/outdoor swimming pool?	¿Hay piscina cubierta/al aire libre?
Is it salt or fresh water?	¿Es agua dulce o salada?
Are there showers?	¿Hay duchas?
I want to hire a cabin for the day/morning/two hours	Quiero alquilar una caseta para todo el día/para la mañana/ por dos horas
I want to hire a deckchair/ sunshade	Quiero alquilar una hamaca/ una sombrilla
Can we water ski here?	¿Se puede hacer aquí ski acuático?
Can we hire the equipment?	¿Se puede alquilar el equipo?
Where's the harbour?	¿Dónde está el puerto?
Can we go out in a fishing boat?	¿Se puede salir en barcos de pesca?
Where can I get skin-diving equipment/flippers?	¿Dónde puedo obtener equipo de natación submarina/aletas?
Can I hire a rowing boat/motor boat?	¿Se puéde alquilar un barco de remo/una motora?
What does it cost by the hour?	¿Cuánto cuesta por hora?

Camping and walking[1]

How long is the walk to the Youth Hostel?	¿Qué distancia hay al Albergue Juvenil?
How far is the next village?	¿A qué distancia está el próximo pueblo?
Is there a footpath to . . . ?	¿Hay camino a . . . ?
Is it possible to go across country?	¿Se puede ir a campo travieso?
Is there a short cut?	¿Hay algún atajo?/¿hay camino más corto?
It's an hour's walk to . . .	*Hay una hora de camino a . . .
Is there a camping site near here?	¿Hay por aquí un camping?
Is this an authorized camp site?	¿Es un camping autorizado?
Is drinking water/are sanitary arrangements/showers provided?	¿Hay agua potable/servicios/duchas?
May we camp here?	¿Se puede acampar aquí?

1. See also DIRECTIONS (p. 48) and HARDWARE (p. 107).

Can we hire a tent?	¿Podemos alquilar una tienda de campaña?
Can we park our caravan here?	¿Podemos poner aquí nuestro remolque?
What does it cost per person/day/week?	¿Qué precio es por persona/día/semana?
What is the charge for a tent/caravan?	¿Qué precio es por una tienda de campaña/caravana?
Is this drinking water?	¿Se puede beber esta agua?
Where are the shops?	¿Dónde están las tiendas?
Where can I buy paraffin/butane gas?	¿Dónde se puede comprar petróleo/butano?
May we light a fire?	¿Se puede hacer fuego?
Where do I dispose of rubbish?	¿Dónde puedo tirar las basuras?

At the doctor's

Ailments

Is there a doctor's surgery nearby?	¿Hay algún dispensario cerca?
I must see a doctor, can you recommend one?	Quiero que me vea un médico, ¿puede recomendarme alguno?
Please call a doctor	Llame al médico, por favor
I am ill	No estoy bien
I have a fever	Tengo calentura
I have a cardiac condition	Sufro del corazón
I've a pain in my right/left arm	Me duele el brazo derecho/izquierdo
My wrist hurts	Me duele la muñeca
I think I've sprained/broken my ankle	Creo que me he dislocado/roto el tobillo

I fell down and my back hurts	Me he caído y me duele la espalda
My foot is swollen	Tengo el pie hinchado
I've burned/cut/bruised myself	Me he quemado/cortado/dado un golpe
My stomach is upset	Tengo mal el estómago
I have indigestion	No hago bien la digestión/tengo indigestión
My appetite's gone	No tengo apetito
I think I've got food poisoning	Creo que estoy intoxicado
I can't eat/sleep	No puedo comer/dormir
I am a diabetic	Soy diabético
My nose keeps bleeding	Sangro por la nariz frecuentemente
I have earache	Me duelen los oídos
I have difficulty in breathing	No respiro bien
I feel dizzy/shivery	Me siento mareado/escalofriado
I feel sick	Tengo nauseas/ganas de devolver
I keep vomiting	Tengo vómitos
I think I've caught 'flu	Creo que tengo gripe
I've got a cold	Tengo catarro
I've had it since yesterday/for a few hours	Lo tengo desde ayer/desde hace unas horas

abscess	el absceso	ab-**sthe**-so
ache	el dolor	do-lor
allergy	la alergia	al-air-hee-a
appendicitis	la apendicitis	apen-dee-thee-tees
asthma	la asma	as-ma
blister	la ampolla	am-poll-ya
boil	el forúnculo	for-**oon**-koo-loh
bruise	el cardenal	car-day-nal
burn	la quemadura	ke-mah-doo-rah
chill	el enfriamiento	en-free-amyen-toh
cold	el catarro	ka-tar-roh
constipation	el estreñimiento	es-tren-yee-myen-toh
cough	la tos	toss
cramp	el calambre	ka-lam-bray
diabetic	diabético	dya-**be**-tee-koh
diarrhoea	la colitis	ko-lee-tees
earache	el dolor de oídos	do-lor de o-ee-dos
fever	la fiebre	fye-breh
food poisoning	la intoxicación	een-tok-see-ka-**thyon**
fracture	la fractura	frak-too-ra
hay-fever	la fiebre del heno	fye-breh del eno
headache	el dolor de cabeza	do-lor de ka-be-tha
ill, sick	enfermo	en-fair-moh
illness	la enfermedad	en-fair-mee-da

indigestion	la indigestión	een-dee-hes-**tyon**
infection	la infección	een-fek-**thyon**
influenza	la gripe	gree-pe
insomnia	el insomnio	een-som-nyoh
nausea	la náusea	**now**-se-ah
pain	el dolor	do-lor
rheumatism	el reumatismo	ray-oom-at-ees-mo
sore throat	la garganta irritada	gar-gan-ta ee-ree-ta-da
stomach ache	el dolor de estómago	do-lor de es-**toh**-ma-go
sunburn	la quemadura de sol	ke-mah-doo-rah de sol
sunstroke	la insolación	een-so-la-**thyon**
toothache	el dolor de muelas	do-lor de mwe-las
ulcer	la úlcera	**ool**-ther-ah
wound	la herida	ay-ree-dah

Treatment

Do you have a temperature?	*¿Tiene algo de temperatura?
Where does it hurt?	*¿Dónde le duele?
Have you a pain here?	*¿Le duele aquí?
How long have you had the pain?	*¿Desde cuándo le duele?
Open your mouth	*Abra la boca
Put out your tongue	*Saque la lengua

Breathe in	*Respire fuerte
Breathe out	*Espire
Does that hurt?	* ¿Le duele eso?
A lot?	* ¿Mucho?
A little?	* ¿Un poco?
Please lie down	*Échese
I will need a specimen	*Necesito un espécimen
What medicines have you been taking?	* ¿Qué medicinas ha estado tomando?
I take this medicine; could you give me another prescription?	Tomo estas medicinas; podría recetármelas?
I'll give you some pills/ medicine	*Voy a darle unas píldoras/una medicina
I will give you an antibiotic/ sedative	*Le daré un antibiótico/un sedante
Are you allergic to antibiotics?	* ¿Es usted alérgico a los antibióticos?
Take this prescription to the chemist's .	*Lleve esta receta a la farmacia
Take this three times a day	*Tome la medicina tres veces al día
I'll give you an injection	*Voy a ponerle una inyección
Roll up your sleeve	*Levántese la manga
I'll put you on a diet	*Voy a ponerle un régimen
Come and see me again in two days' time	*Vuelva dentro de dos días

You must be X-rayed	*Hay que hacerle una radiografía
You must go to hospital	*Tiene usted que ir a un hospital/una clínica
You're hurting me	Me hace daño
Must I stay in bed?	¿Tengo que estar en la cama?
Will you call again?	¿Volverá usted?
When can I travel again?	¿Cuándo podré viajar?
You should not travel until ...	*No debiera viajar hasta ...
Nothing to worry about	*No tiene nada para preocuparse
I feel better now	Estoy mejor
How much do I owe you?	¿Cuánto le debo?

ambulance	la ambulancia	am-boo-lan-thya
anaesthetic	el anestésico	anes-tes-ee-ko
aspirin	la aspirina	as-pee-ree-na
bandage	la venda	ben-da
chiropodist	el pedicuro	pe-dee-koo-ro
hospital	el hospital	os-pee-tal
injection	la inyección	een-yek-thyon
laxative	el laxante	lak-san-te
nurse	la enfermera	en-fair-mair-a
operation	la operación	o-pair-a-thyon
optician	el óptico	op-tee-ko

pill	la píldora	**peel-dora**
(adhesive) plaster	el esparadrapo	**es-pa-ra-dra-po**
prescription	la receta	**re-the-ta**
X-ray	la radiografía	**ra-dyo-gra-fee-a**

Parts of the body

ankle	el tobillo	to-bee-llyo
arm	el brazo	bra-tho
back	la espalda	es-pal-da
bladder	la vesícula	bes-ee-koo-la
blood	la sangre	san-gre
body	el cuerpo	kwair-po
brain	el seso	se-so
cheek	la mejilla	me-hee-llya
chest	el pecho	pe-cho
chin	la barbilla	bar-bee-llya
ear	la oreja	or-ay-ha
elbow	el codo	ko-doh
eye	el ojo	o-ho
face	la cara	ka-ra
finger	el dedo	de-doh

foot	el pie	pee-ay
forehead	la frente	fren-te
gums	la encía	en-**thee**-a
hand	la mano	ma-no
head	la cabeza	cab-ay-tha
heart	el corazón	ko-ra-**thon**
heel	el talón	ta-**lon**
hip	la cadera	ka-dair-a
jaw	la mandíbula	man-**dee**-boo-la
kidney	el riñón	reen-yon
knee	la rodilla	ro-dee-llya
knee cap	la rótula	**ro**-too-la
leg	la pierna	pee-air-na
lip	el labio	la-bee-o
liver	el hígado	**ee**-ga-doh
lung	el pulmón	pool-**mon**
mouth	la boca	bo-ka
muscle	el músculo	**moos**-koo-lo
nail	la uña	oon-ya
neck	el cuello	kwe-llyo
nerve	el nervio	nair-byo
nose	la nariz	na-reeth
rib	la costilla	kos-tee-llya
shoulder	la espalda	es-pal-da

skin	la piel	pee-el
stomach	el estómago	es-toh-ma-go
thigh	el muslo	moos-lo
throat	la garganta	gar-gan-ta
thumb	el pulgar	pool-gar
toe	el dedo del pie	de-doh del pee-ay
tongue	la lengua	len-gwa
tonsils	las amígdalas	a-meeg-da-las
tooth	el diente	dyen-te
vein	la vena	be-na
wrist	la muñeca	moon-ye-ka

At the dentist's

I must see a dentist	Quiero ir al dentista
Can I make an appointment?	¿Pueden darme hora?
As soon as possible	Lo antes posible
I have toothache	Me duelen las muelas
This tooth hurts	Me duele este diente
I've lost a filling	Se me ha caído un empaste
Can you fill it?	¿Puede empastarme?
Can you do it now?	¿Puede hacérmelo ahora?
Will you take the tooth out?	¿Tiene que sacarme la muela?
I do not want the tooth taken out	No quiero sacarme el diente
Please give me an injection first	Con inyección, por favor
My gums are swollen/keep bleeding	Tengo las encías inflamadas/ me sangran las encías
I have broken my dentures	Se me ha roto la dentadura
Can you fix it (temporarily)?	¿Puede arreglármelo (temporalmente)?

You're hurting me	Me está haciendo mucho daño
How much do I owe you?	¿Cuánto es, por favor?
When should I come again?	¿Cuándo tengo que volver?
Please rinse your mouth	*Enjuáguese
I will X-ray your teeth	*Tengo que hacerle una radiografía
You have an abscess	*Tiene usted un absceso
The nerve is exposed	*El nervio está al aire
This tooth can't be saved	*Esta muela no se puede salvar

Problems and accidents

Where's the police station?	¿Dónde está la comisaria?
Call the police	Llame a la policía
Where is the British consulate?	¿Dónde está el consulado inglés?
Please let the consulate know	Comuniquen con el consulado
My bag has been stolen	Me han robado el bolso
I found this in the street	He encontrado esto en la calle
I have lost my luggage/ passport/traveller's cheques	He perdido mi equipaje/ mi pasaporte/mis cheques de viajero
I have missed my train	He perdido el tren
My luggage is on board	Mi equipaje está en el tren
Call a doctor	Llame a un médico
Call an ambulance	Llame una ambulancia
There has been an accident	Ha habido un accidente
We've had an accident	Hemos tenido un accidente
He's badly hurt	Está gravemente herido

He has fainted

He's losing blood

Please get some water/a blanket/
some bandages

I've broken my glasses

I can't see

A child has fallen in the water

A woman is drowning

May I see your insurance
certificate?

Apply to the insurance company

Can you help me?

What is the name and address
of the owner?

Are you willing to act as a
witness?

Can I have your name and address
please?

Está sin conocimiento

Está perdiendo sangre

(Tráiganos) agua/una manta/
vendas, por favor

Se me han roto las gafas

No veo

Se ha caído al agua un niño

Se está ahogando una mujer

*Quiero ver su póliza de seguros

Diríjase a la compañía de
seguros

¿Puede ayudarme?

¿Cuál es el nombre y dirección
del propietario?

¿Está usted dispuesto a servir
de testigo?

¿Su nombre y dirección, por
favor?

Time and dates

TIME

What time is it?	¿Qué hora es?
It's one o'clock	Es la una
two o'clock	Son las dos
quarter to ten	Son las diez menos cuarto
quarter past five	las cinco y cuarto
half past four	las cuatro y media
five past eight	las ocho y cinco
twenty to three	las tres menos veinte
twenty-five to seven	las siete menos veinticinco
twenty-five past eight	las ocho y veinticinco
Second	el segundo
Minute	el minuto
Hour	la hora
It's early/late	Es temprano/tarde

My watch is slow/fast	Mi reloj está atrasado/ adelantado
The clock has stopped	Se ha parado el reloj
Sorry I am late	Perdone mi retraso

DATE

What's the date?	¿A cuántos estamos?/ ¿qué día es hoy?
It's December 9th[1]	Hoy es el nueve de diciembre
We're leaving on January 5th	Nos marchamos el cinco de enero
We got here on July 27th	Llegamos el veintisiete de julio

DAY	EL DÍA	dee-a
Morning	la mañana	ma-nya-na
this morning	esta mañana	es-ta ma-nya-na
in the morning	por la mañana	por la ma-nya-na
Midday, noon	mediodía	me-dyo-**dee**-a
Afternoon	la tarde	tar-de
yesterday afternoon	ayer por la tarde	a-yair por la tar-de
Dusk, nightfall[2]	el anochecer	a-no-che-thair

1. Cardinal numbers are used for dates in Spanish, except for 1st which is *primero*.
2. Spanish has no exact equivalent of the English word 'evening': *la tarde* is used if the time is before sunset; *la noche* if it is after.

Midnight	medianoche	me-dya-no-che
Night	la noche	no-che
tonight	esta noche	es-ta no-che
tomorrow night	mañana por la noche	ma-nya-na por la no-che
Sunrise	el amanecer	a-ma-ne-thair
Dawn	la madrugada	ma-droo-ga-da
Sunset, twilight	el crepúsculo	cre-poo-scoo-lo
Today	hoy	oy
Yesterday	ayer	a-yair
day before yesterday	anteayer	an-te-a-yair
Tomorrow	mañana	ma-nya-na
day after tomorrow	pasado mañana	pa-sa-doh ma-nya-na
In ten days' time	dentro de diez días	den-troh de dyeth dee-as

WEEK	LA SEMANA	se-ma-na
Sunday	domingo	doh-meen-go
Monday	lunes	loo-nes
Tuesday	martes	mar-tes
Wednesday	miércoles	myair-ko-les
Thursday	jueves	hwe-bes

s.p.b. – 7

Friday	viernes	byair-nes
Saturday	sábado	sa-ba-doh
on Tuesday	el martes	el mar-tes
on Sundays	los domingos	los doh-meen-gos
Fortnight	quince días/	keen-theh dee-as
	dos semanas	dos se-ma-nas

MONTH	**EL MES**	mes
January	enero	e-nair-oh
February	febrero	feb-rair-oh
March	marzo	mar-tho
April	abril	ab-reel
May	mayo	ma-oh
June	junio	hoo-nyo
July	julio	hoo-lyo
August	agosto	agos-toh
September	setiembre	se-tyem-bre
October	octubre	ok-too-bre
November	noviembre	no-byem-bre
December	diciembre	dee-thyem-bre

SEASON	**LA TEMPORADA**	tem-po-ra-da
Spring	la primavera	pree-ma-bair-a
Summer	el verano	bair-ra-no

Autumn	el otoño	oton-yo
Winter	el invierno	een-byair-noh
in spring	en primavera	en pree-ma-bair-a
during the summer	durante el verano	doo-ran-te el bai-ra-no

YEAR	EL AÑO	an-yo
This year	este año	es-te an-yo
Last year	el año pasado	el an-yo pa-sa-doh
Next year	el próximo año/el año que viene	el pro-see-mo an-yo/el an-yo kay bye-ne

Public holidays

1 January	Año nuevo	New Year's Day
6 January	Día de Reyes	Epiphany
19 March	Sán José	St Joseph's Day
Good Friday	Viernes santo	
Ascension Day	Día de la Asención	
Corpus Christi	Corpus Cristi	
25 July	Día de Santiago (patron saint of Spain)	St James's Day
15 August	Día de la Asunción	Assumption Day

12 October	Fiesta de la Hispanidad	Columbus Day
1 November	Todos los Santos	All Saints Day
8 December	Inmaculada Concepción	Immaculate Conception Day
25 December	Navidad	Christmas

Apart from these holidays every town and village celebrates its own holiday which usually coincides with the day of its patron saint.

Numbers

CARDINAL

0	cero	the-ro
1	uno/un, una	oo-no/oon, oo-na
2	dos	dos
3	tres	tres
4	cuatro	kwa-tro
5	cinco	theen-ko
6	seis	says
7	siete	sye-te
8	ocho	ocho
9	nueve	nwe-be
10	diez	dyeth
11	once	on-the
12	doce	do-the
13	trece	tre-the
14	catorce	ka-tor-the

15	quince	keen-the
16	diez y seis/dieciseis	dyeth ee says
17	diez y siete/diecisiete	dyeth ee sye-te
18	diez y ocho/dieciocho	dyeth ee ocho
19	diez y nueve/ diecinueve	dyeth ee nwe-be
20	veinte	beyn-te
21	veintiuno	ben-tee-oo-no
22	veintidos	ben-tee-dos
30	treinta	tre-een-ta
31	treinta y uno	tre-een-ta-ee-oo-no
40	cuarenta	kwa-ren-ta
41	cuarenta y uno	kwa-ren-ta-ee-oo-no
50	cincuenta	theen-kwen-ta
51	cincuenta y uno	theen-kwen-ta-ee-oo-no
60	sesenta	se-sen-ta
61	sesenta y uno	se-sen-ta-ee-oo-no
70	setenta	se-ten-ta
71	setenta y uno	se-ten-ta-ee-oo-no
80	ochenta	o-chen-ta
81	ochenta y uno	o-chen-ta-ee-oo-no
90	noventa	no-ben-ta
91	noventa y uno	no-ben-ta-ee-oo-no
100	cien/ciento	thyen/thyen-toh
101	ciento uno	thyen-toh oo-no

200	doscientos	dos-thyen-tos
500	quinientos	kin-yen-tos
700	setecientos	se-te-thyen-tos
1000	mil	meel
2000	dos mil	dos meel
1,000,000	un millón	mee-**llyon**

ORDINAL

1st	primero/primer, primera	pree-mair-oh/pree-mair, pree-mair-a
2nd	segundo, -a	se-goon-doh
3rd	tercero, -a	tair-thair-oh
4th	cuarto, -a	kwar-toh
5th	quinto, -a	keen-toh
6th	sexto, -a	ses-toh
7th	séptimo, -a	sep-tee-moh
8th	octavo, -a	oc-ta-boh
9th	noveno, -a	no-be-noh
10th	décimo, -a	de-thee-moh

half	medio, -a/la mitad	me-dyo, mee-ta
quarter	un cuarto	kwar-toh
three quarters	tres cuartos	tres kwar-tos
a third	un tercio	tair-thyo
two thirds	dos tercios	dos tair-thyos

Weights and measures

DISTANCE
kilometres – miles

km	miles or km	miles		km	miles or km	miles
1·6	1	0·6		14·5	9	5·6
3·2	2	1·2		16·1	10	6·2
4·8	3	1·9		32·2	20	12·4
6·4	4	2·5		40·2	25	15·3
8	5	3·1		80·5	50	31·1
9·7	6	3·7		160·9	100	62·1
11·3	7	4·4		804·7	500	310·7
12·9	8	5·0				

A rough way to convert from miles to km: divide by 5 and multiply by 8; from km to miles divide by 8 and multiply by 5.

LENGTH AND HEIGHT

centimetres – inches

cm	ins or cm	ins		cm	ins or cm	ins
2·5	1	0·4		17·8	7	2·8
5·1	2	0·8		20	8	3·2
7·6	3	1·2		22·9	9	3·5
10·2	4	1·6		25·4	10	3·9
12·7	5	2·0		50·8	20	7·9
15·2	6	2·4		127	50	19·7

A rough way to convert from inches to cm: divide by 2 and multiply by 5; from cm to inches divide by 5 and multiply by 2.

metres – feet

m	ft or m	ft		m	ft or m	ft
0·3	1	3·3		2·4	8	26·3
0·6	2	6·6		2·7	9	29·5
0·9	3	9·8		3	10	32·8
1·2	4	13·1		6·1	20	65·6
1·5	5	16·4		15·2	50	164
1·8	6	19·7		30·5	100	328·1
2·1	7	23				

A rough way to convert from ft to m: divide by 10 and multiply by 3; from m to ft divide by 3 and multiply by 10.

metres – yards

m	yds or m	yds		m	yds or m	yds
0·9	1	1·1		7·3	8	8·8
1·8	2	2·2		8·2	9	9·8
2·7	3	3·3		9·1	10	10·9
3·7	4	4·4		18·3	20	21·9
4·6	5	5·5		45·7	50	54·7
5·5	6	6·6		91·4	100	109·4
6·4	7	7·7		457·2	500	546·8

A rough way to convert from yds to m: subtract 10 per cent from the number of yds; from m to yds add 10 per cent to the number of metres.

LIQUID MEASURES

litres – gallons

litres	galls or litres	galls		litres	galls or litres	galls
4·6	1	0·2		36·4	8	1·8
9·1	2	0·4		40·9	9	2·0
13·6	3	0·7		45·5	10	2·2
18·2	4	0·9		90·9	20	4·4
22·7	5	1·1		136·4	30	6·6
27·3	6	1·3		181·8	40	8·8
31·8	7	1·5		227·3	50	11

1 pint = 0·6 litre   1 litre = 1·8 pint

A rough way to convert from galls to litres: divide by 2 and multiply by 9; from litres to galls, divide by 9 and multiply by 2.

WEIGHT

kilogrammes – pounds

kg	lb. or kg	lb.	kg	lb. or kg	lb.
0·5	1	2·2	3·2	7	15·4
0·9	2	4·4	3·6	8	17·6
1·4	3	6·6	4·1	9	19·8
1·8	4	8·8	4·5	10	22·1
2·3	5	11·0	9·1	20	44·1
2·7	6	13·2	22·7	50	110·2

A rough way to convert from lb. to kg: divide by 11 and multiply by 5; from kg to lb. divide by 5 and multiply by 11.

grammes – ounces

grammes	oz.	oz.	grammes
100	3·5	2	57·1
250	8·8	4	114·3
500	17·6	8	228·6
1000 (1 kg)	35	16 (1 lb.)	457·2

TEMPERATURE

centigrade (°C) – fahrenheit (°F)

°C	°F
— 10	14
— 5	23
0	32
5	41
10	50
15	59
20	68
25	77
30	86
35	95
37	98·4
38	100·5
39	102
40	104
100	212

To convert °F to °C: deduct 32, divide by 9, multiply by 5; to convert °C to °F: divide by 5, multiply by 9 and add 32.

Vocabulary

Various groups of specialized words are given elsewhere in this book and these words are not usually repeated in the vocabulary:

A

a, an	un, una	oon, oona
able (to be)	poder	po-dair
about	alrededor de	al-re-de-dor de
above	encima (de)	en-thee-ma
abroad	al extranjero	al es-tran-hair-oh
accept (to)	aceptar	a-thep-tar
accident	el accidente	ak-thee-dente
ache (to)	doler	do-lair
acquaintance	el conocido	ko-no-thee-doh
across	a través de	a tra-bes de
act (to)	actuar	ak-too-ar
add	añadir	anya-deer
address	la dirección	dee-rek-thyon
admire (to)	admirar	ad-mee-rar
admission	la admisión/la entrada	ad-mee-syon/en-tra-da
advice	el consejo	kon-say-ho
aeroplane	el avión	ab-yon
afraid (to be)	tener miedo	ten-air myay-doh
after	después (de)	des-pwes
again	otra vez	otra beth
against	contra	kon-tra

age	la edad	ay-da
agency	la agencia	ahen-thya
agent	el agente	ahen-te
agree (to)	estar de acuerdo	es-tar dak-wair-doh
air	el aire	a-ee-re
airbed	el colchón de aire	kol-**chon** da-ee-re
air-conditioning	el aire acondicionado	a-ee-re akon-dee-thyon-adoh
alike	parecido	pa-re-thee-doh
all	todo	toh-doh
allow (to)	permitir	pair-mee-teer
all right	bueno/bien	bway-no/byen
almost	casi	ka-see
alone	solo	so-lo
along	a lo largo	a lo lar-go
already	ya	ya
also	también	tam-**byen**
alter (to)	modificar	mo-dee-fee-kar
alternative	la alternativa	al-tair-na-tee-ba
although	aunque	a-oon-ke
always	siempre	sy-em-pte
ambulance	la ambulancia	am-boo-lan-thya
America	los Estados Unidos	es-ta-dos oo-nee-dos
American	americano	amer-ee-ka-no

among	entre	en-tre
amuse (to)	divertir	dee-bair-teer
amusing	divertido	dee-bair-tee-doh
ancient	antiguo	an-tee-gwo
and	y	ee
angry	enfadado	en-fa-da-doh
animal	el animal	anee-mal
anniversary	el aniversario	anee-bair-sa-ree-o
annoy (to)	molestar	mo-les-tar
another	otro	ot-ro
answer	la respuesta	res-pwes-ta
answer (to)	contestar	kon-tes-tar
antique	antiguo	an-tee-gwo
any *pron.*	alguno	al-goo-no
any *adj.*	algún	al-goon
anyone, someone	alguien	alg-yen
anything, something	algo	al-go
anyway	de todos modos	de toh-dos mo-dos
anywhere, somewhere	en alguna parte	en al-goo-na par-te
apartment	el apartamento	apar-ta-men-toh
apologize (to)	disculpar	dees-kool-par
appetite	el apetito	ap-e-tee-toh
appointment *general*	la cita	thee-ta
appointment *dentist, etc.*	la hora tomada	ora to-ma-da

architect	el arquitecto	ar-kee-**tek**-toh
architecture	la arquitectura	ar-kee-tek-**toora**
argument	la discusión	dees-koo-**syon**
arm	el brazo	bra-tho
armchair	el sillón	see-**llyon**
army	el ejército	e-**hair**-thee-toh
around	alrededor de	al-ray-de-dor de
arrange (to)	arreglar	arreg-lar
arrival	la llegada	llye-ga-da
arrive (to)	llegar	llye-gar
art	el arte	ar-te
art gallery	la galería de arte	gal-air-**ee**-a dar-te
artist	el artista	ar-tees-ta
as	como	ko-mo
as much as	tanto como	tan-toh ko-mo
as soon as	tan pronto como	tan pron-toh ko-mo
as well, also	también	tam-**byen**
ashtray	el cenicero	then-ee-**thair**-oh
ask (to)	preguntar	pre-goon-tar
asleep	dormido	dor-mee-doh
at	en	en
at last	al fin	al feen
at once	en seguida	en se-gee-da

atmosphere	el ambiente	am-byen-te
attention	la atención	aten-**thyon**
attractive	atractivo	a-trak-tee-boh
auction	la subasta/la almoneda	soo-bas-ta/al-mo-ne-da
audience	el auditorio/el público	ow-dee-tor-ee-o/**poo**-blee-ko
aunt	la tía	tee-a
Australia	Australia	ows-tral-ya
Australian	australiano	ows-tral-ya-no
author	el autor	ow-tor
available	disponible	dees-po-nee-ble
average	el término medio	ter-mee-no me-dee-oh
awake	despierto	des-pyair-toh
away	fuera	fwair-a
awful	horrible	or-ree-bleh

B

baby	el niño	nee-nyo
bachelor	el soltero	sol-tair-oh
back *returned*	de vuelta	de bwel-ta
bad	malo	ma-lo
bag	la bolsa	bol-sa

baggage	el equipaje	e-kee-pa-heh
bait *fishing*	el cebo	thay-bo
balcony	el balcón	bal-**kon**
ball *dance*	el baile	ba-ee-le
ball *sport*	la pelota	pe-lo-ta
ballpoint pen	el bolígrafo	bol-ee-gra-fo
band *music*	la orquesta	or-kes-ta
bank	el banco	ban-ko
bare	desnudo/descubierto	des-noo-doh/des-koo-byer-toh
basket	la cesta	thes-ta
bath	el baño	ban-yo
bathe (to)	bañar	ban-yar
bathing cap	el gorro de baño	gor-ro de ban-yo
bathing costume	el traje de baño	tra-he de ban-yo
bathing trunks	el bañador	ban-ya-dor
bathroom	el cuarto de baño	kwar-toh de ban-yo
battery	la batería	ba-tair-ee-a
bay	la bahía	ba-ee-a
be (to)	ser,	sair,
	estar	es-tar
beach	la playa	pla-ya
beard	la barba	bar-ba
beautiful	hermoso	air-mo-so

because	porque	por-ke
become	hacerse	a-thair-se
bed	la cama	ka-ma
bedroom	el dormitorio	dor-mee-tor-yo
before	antes	an-tes
begin (to)	empezar	em-pe-thar
beginning	el principio	preen-thee-pyo
behind	atrás	a-tras
believe (to)	creer	kray-air
bell	la campana	kam-pa-na
belong (to)	pertenecer	pair-ten-e-thair
below	abajo	a-ba-ho
belt	el cinturón	thin-toor-on
bench	el banquillo	ban-kee-llyo
bend	la curva	koor-ba
berth	la litera	lee-tair-a
beside	cerca de/al lado de	thair-ka de/al la-do de
best	el mejor	me-hor
better	mejor	me-hor
between	entre	en-tre
bicycle	la bicicleta	bee-thee-klay-ta
big	grande	gran-de
bill	la factura	fak-too-ra
binoculars	los gemelos	he-me-los

bird	el pájaro	**pa-ha-ro**
birthday	el cumpleaños	**koom-ple-an-yos**
bite (to)	morder	**mor-dair**
bitter	amargo	**a-mar-go**
blanket	la manta	**man-ta**
bleed (to)	sangrar	**san-grar**
blind	ciego	**thee-eh-go**
blind *window*	la persiana	**pair-see-a-na**
blond	rubio	**roo-bee-oh**
blood	la sangre	**san-gre**
blouse	la blusa	**bloo-sa**
blow	el golpe	**gol-peh**
(on) board	a bordo	**a bor-doh**
boarding house	la pensión	**pen-syon**
boat	el barco	**bar-ko**
body	el cuerpo	**kwair-po**
bone	el hueso	**way-so**
bonfire	la hoguera	**o-gair-a**
book	el libro	**lee-bro**
book (to)	reservar	**res-air-bar**
boot	la bota	**bo-ta**
border	la frontera	**fron-tair-a**
borrow (to)	pedir prestado	**pe-deer pres-ta-doh**
both	ambos	**am-bos**

bottle	la botella	bo-te-llya
bottle opener	el abrebotellas	abre-bo-te-llyas
bottom	el fondo	fon-doh
bowl	el tazón	ta-thon
box *container*	la caja	ka-ha
box *theatre*	el palco	pal-ko
box office	la taquilla	ta-kee-llya
boy	el muchacho	moo-cha-cho
bracelet	la pulsera	pool-sair-a
braces	los tirantes	tee-ran-tes
brain	el cerebro	the-re-bro
branch *tree*	la rama	ra-ma
branch *bank, etc.*	la sucursal	soo-koor-sal
brand	la marca	mar-ka
brassière	el sujetador	soo-he-ta-dor
break (to)	romper	rom-pair
breakfast	el desayuno	des-a-yoo-no
breathe (to)	respirar	res-pee-rar
bridge	el puente	pwen-te
briefs	los calzoncillos	kal-thon-thee-llyo
bright *colour*	vivo	bee-bo
bring (to)	traer	tra-air
British	británico	bree-tan-ee-ko
broken	roto	ro-toh

brooch	el broche	bro-che
brother	el hermano	air-ma-no
brush	el cepillo	the-pee-llyo
brush (to)	cepillar	the-pee-llyar
bucket	el cubo	koo-bo
buckle	la hebilla	e-bee-llya
build (to)	construir	kon-strweer
building	el edificio	edee-fee-thyo
bullfight	la corrida de toros	kor-ree-da de to-ros
bullring	la plaza de toros	pla-tha de to-ros
buoy	la boya	bo-ya
burn (to)	quemar	ke-mar
burst (to)	reventar	re-ben-tar
bus	el autobús	ow-toh-**boos**
bus stop	la parada	pa-ra-da
business	el negocio	ne-go-thyo
busy	ocupado	okoo-pa-do
but	pero	pe-ro
button	el botón	bo-ton
buy (to)	comprar	kom-prar
by	por	por

C

cabin	el camarote	ka-ma-ro-te
cable	el telegrama	te-le-grama
call (to) *summon, name*	llamar	llya-mar
(telephone) call	la llamada (telefónica)	llya-mada tele-**fon**-ee-ka
call (to) *visit*	visitar	bee-see-tar
call *visit*	la visita	bee-see-ta
calm	tranquillo	tran-kee-lo
camera	la máquina fotográfica	ma-kee-na foto-**gra**-fee-ka
camp (to)	acampar	akam-par
camp site	el camping	kam-peeng
can (to be able)	poder	po-dair
can *tin*	la lata	la-ta
Canada	Canadá *m*	ka-na-**da**
Canadian	canadiense	ka-na-dyen-se
cancel (to)	anular	a-noo-lar
candle	la vela	be-la
canoe	la canoa	ka-no-a
cap	la gorra	gor-ra
capital city	la capital	ka-pee-tal
car	el coche	ko-che

car park	el estacionamiento	es-ta-thyon-a-myen-toh
caravan	el remolque	re-mol-ke
card	la tarjeta	tar-he-ta
(playing) card	la carta	kar-ta
care	el cuidado	kwee-da-do
careful	cuidadoso	kwee-da-do-so
careless	descuidado	des-kwee-da-do
carry (to)	llevar	llye-bar
cash (to)	cambiar	kam-byar
cashier	el cajero	ka-hair-oh
casino	el casino	ka-see-no
castle	el castillo	kas-tee-llyo
cat	el gato	ga-toh
catalogue	el catálogo	ka-ta-lo-go
catch (to)	coger	ko-hair
cathedral	la catedral	ka-te-dral
catholic	católico	ka-toh-lee-ko
cause	la causa	kow-sa
cave	la cueva	kwe-ba
central	central	then-tral
centre	el centro	then-tro
century	el siglo	see-glo
ceremony	la ceremonia	the-re-mon-ya

certain	seguro	se-goo-ro
certainly	ciertamente	thyair-ta-mente
chair	la silla	see-llya
chambermaid	la camarera	ka-ma-rair-a
chance	la oportunidad	op-or-too-nee-da
(small) change	el dinero suelto	dee-nair-oh swel-toh
change (to)	cambiar	kam-byar
charge	la tarifa	ta-ree-fa
charge (to)	cobrar	kob-rar
cheap	barato	ba-ra-toh
check (to)	examinar	eg-sam-ee-nar
cheque	el cheque	che-ke
child	el niño	nee-nyo
china	la porcelana	por-the-lana
choice	la selección	se-lek-thyon
choose (to)	elegir	el-e-heer
Christmas	la Navidad	na-bee-da
church	la iglesia	ee-gle-sya
cigar	el puro	poo-roh
cigarette	el pitillo,	pee-tee-llyo,
	el cigarrillo	thee-gar-ree-llyo
cigarette case	la pitillera	pee-tee-llyair-a
cigarette lighter	el encendedor	en-then-de-dor
cinema	el cine	thee-ne

circle *theatre*	el anfiteatro	an-fee-te-atro
circus	el circo	theer-ko
city	la ciudad	thyoo-da
class	la clase	kla-se
clean (to)	limpiar	leem-pyar
clean	limpio	leem-pyo
clear	claro	kla-ro
cliff	el acantilado	acan-tee-la-doh
climb	escalar	es-ka-lar
cloakroom	el guardarropa	gwar-dar-ropa
clock	el reloj	re-loh
close (to)	cerrar	ther-rar
closed	cerrado	ther-ra-do
cloth	la tela	te-la
clothes	los trajes	tra-hes
cloud	la nube	noo-beh
coach	el coche	ko-che
coast	la costa	kos-ta
coat	el abrigo	abree-go
coathanger	la percha	pair-cha
coin	la moneda	mo-ne-da
cold	frío	free-oh
cold cream	la crema para la cara	kre-ma para la kara
collar	el cuello	kwe-llyo

collar stud	el pasador	pa-sa-dor
collect (to)	recoger	re-ko-hair
colour	el color	ko-lor
colour film	el carrete de color	kar-re-te de ko-lor
comb	el peine	pe-ee-ne
come (to)	venir	be-neer
come in	¡adelante!	ade-lan-te
comfortable	cómodo	ko-mo-do
common	común	ko-moon
company	la compañía	kom-pan-yee-a
compartment *train*	el departamento	de-par-ta-men-toh
complain (to)	quejarse	ke-har-se
complaint	la queja	ke-ha
complete	completo	kom-ple-toh
concert	el concierto	kon-thyair-toh
condition	la condición	kon-dee-thyon
conductor *bus*	el cobrador	ko-bra-dor
conductor *orchestra*	el director de orquesta	dee-rek-tor de or-kes-ta
congratulations	¡felicidades!	fe-lee-thee-da-des
connect (to) *train, etc.*	enlazar	en-la-thar
connection	la conexión	ko-nek-see-on
consul	el cónsul	kon-sool
consulate	el consulado	kon-sool-adoh
contain (to)	contener	kon-ten-air

contrast	el contraste	kon-tras-te
convenient	conveniente	kon-ben-yen-te
convent	el convento	kon-ben-toh
conversation	la conversación	kon-bair-sa-**thyon**
cook	el cocinero	ko-thee-nair-oh
cook (to)	cocer	ko-thair
cool	fresco	fres-ko
copper *metal*	el cobre	ko-bre
copy	la copia	ko-pee-a
cork	el corcho	kor-cho
corkscrew	el sacacorchos	sa-ka-kor-chos
corner	la esquina	es-kee-na
correct	correcto	kor-rek-toh
corridor	el pasillo	pa-see-llyo
cosmetics	los cosméticos	kos-me-tee-kos
cost	el precio	pre-thyo
cost (to)	costar	kos-tar
cot	la cuna	koo-na
cotton	el algodón	al-go-**don**
cotton wool	el algodón	al-go-**don**
couchette	la litera	lee-tair-a
count (to)	contar	kon-tar
country *nation*	el país	pa-ees
countryside	el campo	kam-po

courtyard	el patio	pa-tyo
cousin	el primo	pree-mo
cover	la cubierta	koo-bee-air-ta
cow	la vaca	ba-ka
credit	el crédito	kre-dee-toh
crew	la tripulación	tree-poo-la-thyon
cross	la cruz	krooth
cross (to)	atravesar	atra-be-sar
crossroads	el cruce de carreteras	kroo-the de kar-re-tair-as
crowd	la multitud	mool-tee-too
cry (to)	llorar	llyo-rar
cufflinks	los gemelos	he-me-los
cup	la taza	ta-tha
cupboard	el armario	ar-ma-ryo
cure (to)	curar	koo-rar
curious	curioso	koo-ree-o-so
curl (to)	rizar	ree-thar
current	la corriente	kor-ryen-te
curtain	la cortina	kor-tee-na
curve	la curva	koor-ba
cushion	el cojín	ko-heen
customs	la duana	a-dwan-a
customs officer	el oficial de aduana	off-ee-thyal da-dwan-a

| cut | la cortadura | kor-ta-doo-ra |
| cut (to) | cortar | kor-tar |

D

daily	diario	dee-ar-yo
damaged	averiado	a-be-rya-doh
damp	húmedo	oo-me-doh
dance	el baile	ba-ee-le
dance (to)	bailar	ba-ee-lar
danger	el peligro	pe-lee-gro
dangerous	peligroso	pe-lee-gro-so
dark	oscuro	os-koo-ro
date	la fecha	fe-cha
date *appointment*	la cita	thee-ta
daughter	la hija	ee-ha
day	el día	dee-a
dead	muerto	mwair-toh
deaf	sordo	sor-doh
dear	caro	ka-ro
decide (to)	decidir	de-thee-deer
deck	la cubierta	koo-byair-ta
deckchair	la hamaca	a-ma-ka
declare (to)	declarar	de-kla-rar

deep	profundo	pro-foon-doh
delay	el retraso	re-tra-so
deliver (to)	entregar	en-tre-gar
delivery	el reparto	re-par-toh
demi-pension	la media pensión	me-dya pen-**syon**
dentist	el dentista	den-tees-ta
deodorant	el desodorante	de-so-dor-an-te
depart (to)	salir	sa-leer
department	el departamento	de-par-ta-men-toh
department store	el almacén	alma-**then**
departure	la salida	sa-lee-da
dessert	el postre	pos-tre
detour	la desviación	des-bya-**thyon**
develop *film*	revelar	re-be-lar
dial (to)	marcar	mar-kar
diamond	el brillante	bree-llyan-te
dice	los dados	da-dos
dictionary	el diccionario	deek-thyo-nar-yo
diet	la dieta	dye-ta
diet (to)	estar a dieta	es-tar a dye-ta
different	differente	dee-fair-en-te
difficult	difícil	dee-fee-theel
dine (to)	cenar	the-nar
dining room	el comedor	ko-me-dor

dinner	la cena	the-na
direct	directo	dee-rek-toh
direction	la dirección	dee-rek-**thyon**
dirty	sucio	soo-thyo
disappointed	decepcionado	de-thep-thee-on-a-doh
discothèque	la discoteca	dees-ko-te-ka
dish	el plato	pla-toh
disinfectant	el desinfectante	de-seen-fek-tan-te
distance	la distancia	dees-tan-thya
disturb (to)	molestar	mo-les-tar
ditch	la cuneta	koo-ne-ta
dive (to)	tirarse de cabeza	tee-rar-se de ka-be-tha
diving board	el trampolín	tram-po-**leen**
divorced	divorciado	dee-bor-thya-doh
do (to)	hacer	a-thair
dock (to)	atracar	atra-kar
doctor	el médico	**me**-dee-ko
dog	el perro	per-ro
doll	la muñeca	moon-ye-ka
door	la puerta	pwair-ta
double	doble	do-ble
double bed	la cama doble	ka-ma do-ble
double room	la habitación de matrimonio	abee-ta-**thyon** de mat-ree-mo-nyo

down (stairs)	abajo	a-ba-ho
dozen	la docena	do-the-na
drawer	el cajón	ka-hon
dream	el sueño	swen-yo
dress	el vestido	bes-tee-doh
dressing gown	la bata	ba-ta
dressmaker	la modista	mo-dees-ta
drink (to)	beber	be-bair
drinking water	el agua potable	ag-wa po-ta-ble
drive (to)	conducir	kon-doo-theer
driver	el conductor	kon-dook-tor
drop (to)	dejar caer	de-har ka-yer
drunk	borracho	bor-ra-cho
dry (to)	secar	se-kar
during	mientras	myen-tras

E

each	cada	ka-da
early	temprano	tem-pra-no
earrings	los pendientes	pen-dyen-tes
east	el este	es-te
easy	fácil	fa-theel
eat (to)	comer	ko-mair

edge	el borde	bor-de
elastic	el elástico	e-las-tee-ko
electric light bulb	la bujía eléctrica	boo-hee-a el-ek-tree-ka
electric point	el enchufe	en-choo-fe
electricity	la electricidad	el-ek-tree-thee-da
elevator	el escensor	asen-sor
embassy	la embajada	em-ba-ha-da
emergency exit	la salida de emergencia	sa-lee-da dem-air-hen-thya
empty	vacío	ba-thee-oh
end	el fin	feen
engaged *people*	comprometido	kom-prom-e-tee-doh
engaged *telephone*	ocupado	o-koo-pa-doh
engine	el motor, la máquina	mo-tor, **ma-kee-na**
England	Inglaterra *f*	een-gla-ter-ra
English	inglés	een-**gles**
enjoy oneself (to)	divertirse	dee-bair-teer-se
enlargement	la ampliación	amp-lya-**thyon**
enough	bastante	bas-tan-te
enquiries	la información	een-for-ma-**thyon**
enter (to)	entrar	en-trar
entrance	la entrada	en-tra-da
envelope	el sobre	so-bre
equipment	el equipo	e-kee-po

escape (to)	escapar	es-ka-par
Europe	Europa *f*	ew-ro-pa
even *opp. odd*	igual	ee-gwal
even *smooth*	liso	lee-so
event	el suceso	soo-the-so
every	cada	ka-da
everybody	todos	toh-dos
everything	todo	toh-doh
everywhere	en todas partes	en toh-das par-tes
example	el ejemplo	e-hem-plo
excellent	excelente	eks-the-len-te
except	excepto	eks-thep-toh
excess	el exceso	eks-the-soh
exchange (bureau)	la casa de cambio	ka-sa de kam-byo
exchange rate	el cambio	kam-byo
excursion	la excursión	es-koor-syon
exhibition	la exposición	es-po-see-thyon
exit	la salida	sa-lee-da
expect (to)	esperar	es-pair-ar
expensive	caro	ka-ro
express	urgente	oor-hen-te
express train	el rápido	ra-pee-doh
eye	el ojo	o-ho
eye shadow	la sombra de ojos	som-bra do-hos

F

fabric	la tela	te-la
face	la cara	ka-ra
fact	el hecho	e-cho
factory	la fábrica	**fab-ree-ka**
fade (to)	decolorar	de-ko-lor-ar
faint (to)	desmayarse	des-ma-yar-se
fair *fête*	la feria	fe-rya
fair *blond*	rubio	roo-byo
fall (to)	caer	ka-air
family	la familia	fa-mee-lya
far	lejos	le-hos
fare	el billete	bee-llye-te
farm	la finca	feen-ka
farmer	el agricultor	a-gree-kool-tor
farther	más lejos	mas le-hos
fashion	la moda	mo-da
fast	rápido	**ra-pee-doh**
fat	gordo	gor-doh
father	el padre	pa-dre
fault	la culpa	kool-pa
fear	el temor	te-mor
feed (to)	dar de comer	dar de ko-mer

feel (to)	sentir	sen-teer
female *adj.*	femenino	fe-me-nee-no
fetch (to)	buscar	boos-kar
few	pocos	po-kos
fiancé(e)	el novio (la novia)	no-bee-o(a)
field	el campo	kam-po
fight (to)	luchar	loo-char
fill (to)	llenar	llye-nar
film *camera*	el carrete	kar-re-te
film *cinema*	la película	pe-lee-koo-la
find (to)	hallar	a-llyar
fine	la multa	mool-ta
finish (to)	acabar	a-ka-bar
finished	acabado	a-ka-ba-doh
fire	el fuego	fwe-go
fire escape	la salida de urgencia	sa-lee-da door-hen-thee-a
first	primero	pree-mair-oh
first aid	los primeros auxilios	pree-mer-os ow-see-lyos
first class	la primera (clase)	pree-mair-a kla-se
fish	el pescado	pes-ka-doh
fish (to)	pescar	pes-kar
fisherman	el pescador	pes-ka-dor

fishing tackle	el aparejo de pescar	a-pa-re-ho de pes-kar
fit (to)	sentar	sen-tar
flag	la bandera	ban-dair-a
flat *level*	llano	llya-no
flat	el apartamento	apar-ta-men-toh
flight	el vuelo	bwe-loh
flint *lighter*	la piedra	pye-dra
flippers	las aletas	a-le-tas
float (to)	flotar	flo-tar
flood	la inundación	ee-noon-da-**thyon**
floor *storey*	el piso	pee-so
floor *room*	el suelo	swe-lo
floor show	el espectáculo	es-pek-ta-koo-lo
flower	la flor	flor
fly	la mosca	mos-ka
fly (to)	volar	bo-lar
fold (to)	doblar	dob-lar
follow (to)	seguir	se-geer
food	la comida	ko-mee-da
foot	el pie	pee-ay
football	el fútbol	**foot**-bol
footpath	el camino	ka-mee-no
for	por/para	por/pa-ra
foreign	extranjero	es-tran-hair-o

forest	la selva	sel-ba
forget (to)	olvidar	ol-bee-dar
fork	el tenedor	te-ne-dor
forward	adelante	ade-lan-te
fountain	la fuente	fwen-te
fragile	frágil	**fra**-heel
free	libre/gratuito	lee-bre/gra-twee-toh
fresh	fresco	fres-ko
fresh water	el agua dulce	ag-wa dool-the
friend	el amigo	amee-go
from	de/desde	de/des-de
(in) front	frente	fren-te
frontier	la frontera	fron-tair-a
frozen	congelado	kon-hel-ado
fruit	la fruta	froo-ta
full	lleno	llye-no
full board	la pensión completa	pen-**syon** kom-ple-ta
fun	la diversión	dee-bair-**syon**
funny	cómico/divertido	**ko**-mee-ko/dee-bair-tee-doh
fur	la piel	pyel
furniture	los muebles	mwe-bles

G

gallery	la galería	ga-lair-ee-a
gamble (to)	jugar	hoo-gar
game	el juego	hwe-go
garage	el garaje	ga-ra-he
garbage	la basura	ba-soo-ra
garden	el jardín	har-**deen**
gas	el gas	gas
gate	la entrada	en-tra-da
gentlemen	caballeros/señores	ka-ba-llye-ros/ sen-yor-es
get (to)	obtener	ob-te-nair
get off (to)	bajarse	ba-har-se
get on (to)	subirse	soo-beer-se
gift	el regalo	re-ga-lo
girdle	la faja/tubular	fa-ha/too-boo-lar
girl	la muchacha	moo-cha-cha
give (to)	dar	dar
glad	contento	kon-ten-toh
glass	el vaso	ba-so
glasses	las gafas	ga-fas
gloomy	triste	trees-te
glorious	magnífico	mag-**nee**-fee-ko

gloves	los guantes	gwan-tes
go (to)	ir	eer
God	Dios	dyos
gold	el oro	o-ro
good	bueno	bwe-no
government	el gobierno	go-byair-no
granddaughter	la nieta	nye-ta
grandfather	el abuelo	abwe-lo
grandmother	la abuela	abwe-la
grandson	el nieto	nye-to
grass	la hierba	yer-ba
grateful	agradecido	ag-ra-de-thee-doh
gravel	la grava	gra-ba
great	grande	gran-de
groceries	comestibles	ko-mes-tee-bles
ground	el terreno	ter-re-no
grow	crecer	kre-thair
guarantee	la garantía	ga-ran-tee-a
guard	el guardia	gwar-dee-a
guest	el huésped	wes-ped
guide	el guía	gee-a
guide book	la guía	gee-a

hail	el granizo	gra-nee-tho
hair	el pelo	pe-lo
hair brush	el cepillo para el pelo	the-pee-llyo para el pe-lo
hairgrips, hairpins	las horquillas	or-kee-llyas
half	medio	me-dyo
half board	la media pensión	me-dya pen-syon
half fare	el medio billete	me-dyo bee-llye-te
hammer	el martillo	mar-tee-llyo
handbag	el bolso	bol-so
handkerchief	el pañuelo	pan-ywe-lo
hang (to)	colgar	kol-gar
hanger	la percha	pair-cha
happen (to)	suceder	soo-the-dair
happy	feliz	fe-leeth
happy birthday	felicidades	fe-lee-thee-da-des
harbour	el puerto	pwair-toh
hard	duro	doo-ro
hat	el sombrero	som-brair-oh
have (to)	tener	te-nair
have to (to)	deber	de-bair
he	él	el

health	la salud	sa-lood
hear (to)	oír	o-eer
heart	el corazón	ko-ra-thon
heat	el calor	ka-lor
heating	la calefacción	ka-le-fak-**thyon**
heavy	pesado	pe-sa-doh
heel *shoe*	el tacón	ta-kon
height	la altura	al-too-ra
help	la ayuda	a-yoo-da
help (to)	ayudar	a-yoo-dar
her *adj.*	su	soo
hers/his	suyo/suya	soo-yo(a)
here	aquí	a-kee
high	alto	al-toh
hill	la colina	ko-lee-na
hire (to)	alquilar	al-kee-lar
his	su/suyo	soo/soo-yo
hitch hike (to)	hacer auto-stop	a-thair ow-toh-stop
hold (to)	tener	te-nair
hole	el agujero	a-goo-hair-o
holiday	el día de fiesta	**dee**-a de fyes-ta
holidays	las vacaciones	ba-ka-thyo-nes
hollow	hueco	we-ko
(at) home	en casa	en ka-sa

honeymoon	el viaje de novios	bee-a-he de no-bee-os
hope	la esperanza	es-pair-an-tha
horse	el caballo	ka-ba-llyo
horse races	las carreras de caballos	kar-rair-as de ka-ba-llyos
horse riding	el paseo a caballo	pa-se-o a ka-ba-llyo
hospital	el hospital	os-pee-tal
hot	caliente	kal-yen-te
hotel	el hotel	o-tel
hotel keeper	el gerente	he-ren-te
hot water bottle	la bolsa (de agua caliente)	bol-sa
hour	la hora	or-a
house	la casa	ka-sa
how?	¿cómo?	ko-mo
how much/many?	¿cuánto?/¿cuántos?	kwan-to(s)
hungry (to be)	tener hambre	te-nair am-bre
hurry (to)	darse prisa	dar-se pree-sa
hurt (to)	doler	do-lair
husband	el marido	ma-ree-doh

I

I	yo	yo
if	si	see
ill	enfermo	en-fair-moh
immediately	inmediatamente	een-me-dya-ta-men-te
important	importante	eem-por-tan-te
in	en	en
include	incluir	een-kloo-eer
included	incluído	een-kloo-ee-do
inconvenient	incómodo	een-ko-mo-do
incorrect	incorrecto	een-kor-rek-to
information (bureau)	(la oficina de) la información	(o-fee-thee-na de) een-for-ma-**thyon**
ink	la tinta	teen-ta
inn	la posada	po-sa-da
insect	el insecto	een-sek-toh
insect bite	la picadura de insecto	pee-ka-doo-ra deen-sek-toh
insect repellant	la crema anti-insectos	kre-ma an-tee een-sek-tohs
inside	dentro (de)	den-troh
instead (of)	en lugar de	en loo-gar-de
insurance	el seguro	se-goo-ro
insure (to)	asegurar	ase-goo-rar

interested	interesado	een-tair-es-ado
interesting	interesante	een-tair-es-an-te
interpreter	el intérprete	een-**tair**-pre-te
into	en/dentro (de)	en/den-tro
introduce (to)	presentar	pre-sen-tar
invitation	la invitación	een-bee-ta-**thyon**
invite (to)	invitar	een-bee-tar
Ireland	Irlanda *f*	eer-lan-da
Irish	irlandés	eer-lan-**des**
iron (to)	planchar	plan-char
island	la isla	ess-la
it	él/ella	el/ellya

J

jacket	la chaqueta	cha-ke-ta
jar	el tarro	tar-ro
jellyfish	la medusa	me-doo-sa
jewellery	las joyas	hoy-as
job	el trabajo	tra-ba-ho
journey	el viaje	bya-he
jug	jarra	har-ra
jump (to)	saltar	sal-tar
jumper	el jersey	hair-say

K

keep (to)	guardar	gwar-dar
key	la llave	llya-be
kick (to)	dar una patada	dar oo-na pa-ta-da
kind	la clase	kla-se
king	el rey	ray
kiss	el beso	be-so
kiss (to)	besar	be-sar
kitchen	la cocina	ko-thee-na
knickers, briefs	las bragas	bra-gas
knife	el cuchillo	koo-chee-llyo
knock (to) *door*	llamar	llya-mar
know (to) *fact*	saber	sa-bair
know (to) *person*	conocer	ko-no-thair

L

label	la etiqueta	etee-ke-ta
lace	el encaje	en-ka-he
ladies	señoras	sen-yor-as
lamp	la lámpara	lam-pa-ra
land	la tierra	tyer-ra

landlord	el propietario	pro-pye-tar-yo
lane	el camino	ka-mee-no
language	el idioma	ee-dyo-ma
large	grande	gran-de
last	último	**ool**-tee-mo
late	tarde	tar-de
laugh (to)	reír	re-**eer**
lavatory	los servicios	sair-bee-thyos
lavatory paper	el papel higiénico	pa-pel ee-**hyen**-ee-ko
law	la ley	lay
lead (to)	conducir	kon-doo-theer
leaf	la hoja	o-ha
learn (to)	aprender	a-pren-dair
leather	la piel/el cuero	pyel/kwair-oh
leave (to) *abandon*	dejar	de-har
leave (to) *go out*	salir	sa-leer
left *opp. right*	izquierdo	eeth-kyair-doh
left luggage	la consigna	kon-see-na
lend (to)	prestar	pres-tar
length	el largo	lar-go
less	menos	me-nos
lesson	la lección	lek-**thyon**
let (to) *rent*	alquilar	al-kee-lar
let (to) *allow*	dejar	de-har

letter	la carta	kar-ta
library	la biblioteca	bee-blyo-te-ka
licence	el permiso	pair-mee-so
life	la vida	bee-da
lift	el ascensor	as-then-sor
light *colour*	claro	kla-ro
light	la luz	looth
lighter	el encendedor	en-then-de-dor
lighter fuel	la gasolina	ga-so-lee-na
lighthouse	el faro	fa-ro
like (to)	querer	ke-rer
line	la línea	lee-ne-a
linen	el hilo	ee-lo
lingerie	la lencería	len-thair-ee-a
lipstick	la barra de labios	bar-ra de la-byos
liquid *adj.* and *noun*	líquido	lee-kee-doh
listen	escuchar	es-koo-char
little	poco	po-ko
live (to)	vivir	bee-beer
local	local	lo-kal
lock (to)	cerrar con llave	ther-rar kon llya-be
long	largo	lar-go
look (to)	mirar	mee-rar
look (to) *seem*	parecer	pa-re-thair

look for (to)	buscar	boos-kar
loose	suelto	swel-toh
lorry	el camión	**ka-myon**
lose (to)	perder	pair-dair
lost property office	la oficina de objetos perdidos	off-ee-thee-na dob-he-tos pair-dee-dos
loud	ruidoso	rwee-doh-so
love (to)	querer	ke-rair
lovely	hermoso	air-mo-so
low	bajo	ba-ho
luggage	el equipaje	e-kee-pa-he
(piece of) luggage	el bulto	bool-toh
lunch	la comida/el almuerzo	ko-mee-da/ al-mwair-tho

M

mad	loco	lo-ko
magazine	la revista	re-bees-ta
maid	la doncella	don-the-llya
mail	el correo	kor-ray-oh
main street	la calle principal	ka-llye preen-thee-pal
make (to)	hacer	a-thair

make love (to)	hacer el amor	a-thair el a-mor
make-up	el maquillaje	ma-kee-llya-he
male *adj.*	masculino	mas-koo-lee-no
man	el hombre	om-bre
manage (to)	arreglárselas	ar-reg-lar-se-las
manager	el director	dee-rek-tor
manicure	la manicura	ma-nee-koo-ra
many	muchos	moo-chos
map	el mapa	ma-pa
marble	el mármol	**mar**-mol
market	el mercado	mair-ka-do
married	casado	ka-sa-do
Mass	la misa	mee-sa
match	la cerilla	the-ree-llya
match *sport*	el partido	par-tee-doh
material	la tela	te-la
mattress	el colchón	kol-chon
maybe	quizás	kee-thas
meal	la comida	ko-mee-da
measurements	las medidas	me-dee-das
meet (to)	encontrar	en-kon-trar
mend (to)	reparar	re-par-rar
menu	el menú	me-**noo**
mess	el desorden	des-or-den

message	el recado	re-ka-doh
metal	el metal	me-tal
middle	el medio	me-dyo
middle-aged	de edad media	de e-da me-dya
middle class	la clase media	cla-se me-dya
mild	suave	swa-be
mine *pron.*	mío/mía	**mee-oh/mee-a**
minute	el minuto	mee-noo-toh
mirror	el espejo	es-pe-ho
Miss	la señorita	sen-yor-ee-ta
miss (to) *train, etc.*	perder	pair-dair
mistake	la equivocación	ekee-bo-ka-**thyon**
mix (to)	mezclar	meth-klar
modern	moderno	mo-dair-no
moment	el momento	mo-men-toh
money	el dinero	dee-nair-oh
money order	el giro postal	hee-ro po-stal
month	el mes	mes
monument	el monumento	mo-noo-men-toh
moon	la luna	loo-na
more	más	mas
most	lo máximo	ma-see-mo
mosquito	el mosquito	mos-kee-toh
mother	la madre	ma-dre

motor	el motor	mo-tor
motor boat	la motora	mo-tor-a
motor cycle	la motocicleta	mo-toh-thee-kle-ta
motor racing	las carreras de coches	kar-rair-as de ko-ches
motorway	la autopista	ow-toh-pees-ta
mountain	la montaña	mon-tan-ya
mouth	la boca	bo-ka
mouthwash	el enjuague	en-hoo-a-ge
Mr	el señor	sen-yor
Mrs	la señora	sen-yor-a
much	mucho	moo-cho
museum	el museo	moo-se-oh
music	la música	moo-see-ka
must (to have to)	deber	de-bair
my	mi	mee

N

nail	el clavo	kla-bo
nail *finger*	la uña	oon-ya
nailbrush	el cepillo de uñas	the-pee-llyo doon-yas
nailfile	la lima	lee-ma
nail polish	la laca	la-ka

name	el nombre	nom-bre
napkin	la servilleta	sair-bee-llye-ta
nappy	el pañal	pan-yal
narrow	estrecho	es-tre-cho
near	cerca	thair-ka
nearly	casi	ka-see
necessary	necesario	ne-the-sa-ryo
necklace	el collar	ko-llyar
need (to)	necesitar	ne-the-see-tar
needle	la aguja	ag-oo-ha
net	la red	re
never	nunca	noon-ka
new	nuevo	nwe-bo
news	las noticias	no-tee-thyas
newspaper	el periódico	pe-ryo-dee-ko
next	próximo	pro-see-mo
nice	bonito	bo-nee-toh
night	la noche	no-che
nightclub	la sala de fiestas	sa-la de fyes-tas
nightdress	el camisón	ka-mee-son
nobody	nadie	na-dye
noisy	ruidoso	rwee-doh-so
none	ninguno	neen-goo-no
north	el norte	nor-te

not	no	no
note *money*	el billete	bee-llye-te
notebook	el cuaderno de notas	kwa-dair-no de no-tas
nothing	nada	na-da
notice	el aviso	a-bee-so
novel	la novela	no-be-la
now	ahora	a-or-a
number	el número	noo-mer-oh
nylon	el nilón	nee-lon

O

occasion	la ocasión	o-ka-syon
occupied	ocupado	okoo-pa-doh
odd *opp. even*	desigual	des-ee-gwal
odd *strange*	raro	ra-ro
of	de	de
offer	la oferta	o-fair-ta
offer (to)	ofrecer	o-fre-thair
office	la oficina	o-fee-thee-na
officer	el oficial	o-fee-thee-al
official *noun*	el funcionario	foon-thee-on-ar-ee-o
official *adj.*	oficial	off-ee-thee-al
often	frecuentemente	fre-kwen-te-men-te

oil	el aceite	a-thay-te
oily	grasiento	gra-syen-toh
ointment	el ungüento	oon-goo-en-toh
old	viejo	bye-ho
olive	la aceituna	a-thay-too-na
on	en/sobre	en/so-bre
once	una vez	oona beth
only	solamente	so-la-men-te
open (to)	abrir	ab-reer
open *pp*	abierto	ab-yair-toh
opening	la abertura	a-bair-too-ra
opera	la ópera	o-pair-a
opportunity	la oportunidad	op-or-too-nee-da
opposite	enfrente (de)	en-fren-te
or	o	o
orchestra	la orquesta	or-kes-ta
order (to)	pedir	pe-deer
ordinary	ordinario	or-dee-na-ryo
other	otro	o-tro
our/ours	nuestro(s)	nwes-tro
out/outside	fuera/afuera	fwe-ra/a-fwe-ra
over	sobre	so-bre
overcoat	el abrigo	ab-ree-go
overnight (to stay)	pasar la noche	pa-sar la no-che

over there	por allí	por a-llyi
owe (to)	deber	de-ber
owner	el propietario	pro-pye-ta-ryo

P

packet	el paquete	pa-ke-te
page	la página	pa-hee-na
paid	pagado	pa-ga-doh
pain	el dolor	do-lor
paint (to)	pintar	peen-tar
painting	la pintura	peen-too-ra
pair	el par	par
palace	el palacio	pa-la-thyo
pale	pálido	pa-lee-doh
paper	el papel	pa-pel
parcel	el paquete	pa-ke-te
park (to)	aparcar	apar-kar
park	el parque	par-ke
part	la parte	par-te
party	la fiesta/el guateque	fee-es-ta/gwa-te-ke
pass (to)	pasar	pa-sar
passenger	el viajero	bya-hair-oh
passport	el pasaporte	pa-sa-por-te

past	el pasado	pa-sa-doh
path	la senda	sen-da
patient	el enfermo	en-fair-mo
pavement	la acera	a-thair-a
pay (to)	pagar	pa-gar
pearl	la perla	per-la
pebble	la piedra	pyed-ra
pedal	el pedal	pe-**dal**
pedestrian	el peatón	pe-a-**ton**
pen	la pluma	ploo-ma
pencil	el lápiz	**la**-peeth
penknife	la navaja	na-ba-ha
people	la gente	hen-te
perfect	perfecto	per-fek-toh
performance	la representación	re-pre-sen-ta-**thyon**
perfume	el perfume	pair-foo-me
perhaps	quizás	kee-**thas**
perishable	corruptible	kor-roop-tee-ble
permit	el permiso	pair-mee-so
permit (to)	permitir	pair-mee-teer
per person	por persona	por pair-so-na
person	la persona	pair-so-na
personal	personal	pair-so-nal
petrol	la gasolina	ga-so-lee-na

petrol station	la gasolinera	ga-so-lee-ne-ra
photograph	la fotografía	fo-toh-gra-fee-a
photographer	el fotógrafo	fo-toh-gra-fo
piano	el piano	pya-no
pick (to)	coger	co-hair
picnic	la merienda	me-ryen-da
picnic (to)	ir de merienda	eer de me-ryen-da
piece	la pieza/el pedazo	pye-tha/pe-da-tho
pier	el muelle	mwe-llye
pillow	la almohada	al-mo-ada
pin	el alfiler	al-fee-lair
(safety) pin	el imperdible	eem-pair-dee-ble
pipe	la pipa	pee-pa
place	el sitio	see-tyo
plan	el plano	pla-no
plant	la planta	plan-ta
plastic	el plástico	plas-tee-ko
plate	el plato	pla-toh
platform	el andén	an-den
play (to)	jugar	hoo-gar
play	la obra de teatro	ob-ra de te-a-tro
player	el jugador	hoo-ga-dor
plenty	bastante	bas-tan-te
pliers	los alicates	a-lee-ka-tes

plug *bath*	el tapón	ta-pon
plug *electric*	el enchufe	en-choo-fe
pocket	el bolsillo	bol-see-llyo
point	la punta	poon-ta
poisonous	venenoso	be-ne-no-so
policeman	el agente de policía	ahen-te de po-lee-thee-a
police station	la comisaría	ko-mee-sa-**ree-a**
poor	pobre	po-bre
popular	popular	po-poo-lar
port	el puerto	pwair-toh
porter	el mozo	mo-tho
possible	posible	po-see-ble
post (to)	echar al correo	e-char al kor-ray-oh
post box	el buzón	boo-**thon**
postcard	la (tarjeta) postal	tar-hay-ta pos-tal
postman	el cartero	kar-tair-oh
post office	(la oficina de) correos	kor-ray-os
postpone (to)	postponer	post-po-nair
pound	la libra	lee-bra
powder *cosmetic*	los polvos	pol-bos
prefer (to)	preferir	pre-fair-eer
prepare (to)	preparar	pre-pa-rar
present *gift*	el regalo	re-ga-lo

press (to)	planchar	plan-char
pretty	bonito	bo-nee-toh
price	el precio	pre-thyo
print (to)	imprimir	eem-pree-meer
private	particular/privado	par-tee-koo-lar/ pree-ba-doh
problem	el problema	pro-ble-ma
profession	la profesión	pro-fe-syon
programme	el programa	pro-gra-ma
promise	la promesa	pro-me-sa
promise (to)	prometer	pro-me-tair
prompt	pronto	pron-toh
protestant	protestante	pro-tes-tan-te
provide (to)	proveer	pro-bay-er
public	público	poo-blee-ko
pull (to)	tirar	tee-rar
pump	la bomba	bom-ba
pure	puro	poo-ro
purse	el monedero	mo-ne-dair-oh
push (to)	empujar	em-poo-har
put (to)	poner	po-nair
pyjamas	el pijama	pee-ha-ma

Q

quality	la calidad	ka-lee-da
quantity	la cantidad	kan-tee-da
quarter	el cuarto	kwar-toh
queen	la reina	re-ee-na
question	la pregunta	pre-goon-ta
queue	la cola	ko-la
queue (to)	ponerse a la cola	po-nair-se a la ko-la
quick	rápido	ra-pee-doh
quiet	tranquilo	tran-kee-lo

R

race	la carrera	kar-re-ra
racecourse	el hipódromo	ee-po-dro-mo
radiator	el radiador	ra-dee-a-dor
radio	la radio	ra-dyo
railway	el ferrocarril	fer-ro-kar-ril
rain	la lluvia	llyoo-bya
(it is) raining	llueve	llyoo-e-be
raincoat	el impermeable	eem-pair-me-a-ble
rare *unusual*	raro	ra-ro

raw	crudo	kroo-doh
razor	la navaja de afeitar	na-ba-ha da-fay-tar
razor blades	las cuchillas de afeitar	koo-chee-llyas da-fay-tar
reach (to)	alcanzar	al-kan-thar
read (to)	leer	lay-er
ready	listo	lees-toh
real	verdadero	bair-da-dair-oh
really	verdaderamente	bair-da-dair-a-men-te
reason	la razón	ra-thon
receipt	el recibo	re-thee-bo
receive (to)	recibir	re-thee-beer
recent	reciente	re-thyen-te
recipe	la receta	re-the-ta
recognize (to)	reconocer	re-kon-o-thair
recommend (to)	recomendar	re-ko-men-dar
record	el disco	dees-ko
record *sport*	el record	re-kord
refrigerator	el refrigerador	re-free-hair-a-dor
register (to)	certificar	thair-tee-fee-kar
relatives	los parientes	pa-ree-en-tes
religion	la religión	re-lee-hee-on
remember (to)	acordarse	akor-dar-se
rent (to)	alquilar	al-kee-lar

repair (to)	arreglar	ar-reg-lar
repeat (to)	repetir	re-pe-teer
reply (to)	contestar	kon-tes-tar
reservation	la reserva	re-sair-ba
reserve (to)	reservar	re-sair-bar
reserved	reservado	re-sair-ba-doh
restaurant	el restaurante	res-tow-ran-te
restaurant car	el coche restaurante	ko-che res-tow-ran-te
return (to)	volver	bol-bair
return (to) *give back*	devolver	de-bol-bair
reward	la recompensa	re-kom-pen-sa
ribbon	la cinta	theen-ta
rich	rico	ree-ko
ride	paseo a caballo	pa-se-o a ka-ba-llyo
ride (to)	montar a caballo	mon-tar a ka-ba-llyo
right *opp. wrong*	correcto	kor-rek-toh
right *opp. left*	derecho	de-re-cho
ring	el anillo	anee-llyo
ripe	maduro	ma-doo-ro
rise (to)	levantar	le-ban-tar
river	el río	**ree-oh**
road	la carretera	kar-re-tair-a
rock	la roca	ro-ka
roll (to)	rodar	ro-dar

rollers *hair*	los rulos	roo-los
roof	el tejado	te-ha-doh
room	la habitación	abee-ta-**thyon**
rope	la soga	so-ga
rotten	podrido	po-dree-do
rough *sea*	agitado	a-hee-ta-doh
rough *surface*	áspero	**as**-pair-o
round	redondo	re-don-do
rowing boat	la barca	bar-ka
rubber	la goma	go-ma
rubbish	la basura	ba-soo-ra
rucksack	la mochila	mo-chee-la
ruin	la ruina	roo-ee-na
rule (to)	gobernar	go-bair-nar
run (to)	correr	kor-rair

S

sad	triste	trees-te
safe	seguro	se-goo-ro
sailor	el marinero	ma-ree-nair-o
sale *clearance*	el saldo/las rebajas	sal-doh/re-ba-has
(for) sale	se vende	se ben-de
salesgirl	la vendedora	ben-de-doh-ra

salesman	el vendedor	ben-de-dor
salt water	el agua salada *f*	ag-wa sa-la-da
same	mismo	mees-mo
sand	la arena	a-re-na
sandals	las sandalias	san-da-lyas
sanitary towels	las compresas (higiénicas)	kom-pre-sas ee-**hyen**-ee-kas
satisfactory	satisfactorio	sa-tees-fak-tor-ee-o
saucer	el platillo	pla-tee-llyo
save (to)	salvar	sal-bar
save (to) *money*	ahorrar	a-or-rar
say (to)	decir	de-theer
scald (to)	quemarse	ke-mar-se
scarf	la bufanda	boo-fan-da
scenery	la vista	bees-ta
scent	el perfume	pair-foo-me
school	la escuela	es-kwe-la
scissors	las tijeras	tee-hair-as
Scotland	Escocia *f*	es-ko-thya
Scottish	escocés	es-ko-**thes**
scratch (to)	arañar	a-ran-yar
screw	el tornillo	tor-nee-llyo
screwdriver	el destornillador	des-tor-nee-llya-dor
sculpture	la escultura	es-kool-too-ra

sea	el mar	mar
seasick	mareado	ma-re-adoh
season	la temporada	tem-po-ra-da
seat	el asiento	a-see-en-toh
second	segundo	se-goon-doh
second class	la segunda (clase)	se-goon-da kla-se
see (to)	ver	bair
seem (to)	parecer	pa-re-thair
sell (to)	vender	ben-dair
send (to)	mandar	man-dar
separate	separado	se-pa-ra-doh
serious	serio	sair-yo
serve (to)	servir	sair-beer
service	el servicio	sair-bee-thyo
service *church : R.C.*	el culto	kool-toh
Prot.	el servicio	sair-bee-thyo
several	varios	bar-yos
sew (to)	coser	ko-sair
shade *colour*	el matiz	ma-teeth
shade *sun*	la sombra	som-bra
shallow	poco profundo	po-ko pro-foon-doh
shampoo	el champú	cham-**poo**
shape	la forma	for-ma
share (to)	repartir	re-par-teer

sharp	agudo	agoo-doh
shave (to)	afeitar	a-fay-tar
shaving brush	la brocha de afeitar	bro-cha da-fay-tar
shaving cream	la crema de afeitar	kre-ma da-fay-tar
she	ella	ellya
sheet	la sábana	sa-ba-na
shell	la concha	kon-cha
shine (to)	brillar	bree-llyar
shingle *beach*	el guijarro	gee-har-ro
ship	el barco	bar-ko
shipping line	la línea marítima	lee-ne-a ma-**ree**-tee-ma
shirt	la camisa	ka-mee-sa
shock	la impresión	eem-pre-**syon**
shoelaces	los cordones de zapatos	kor-doh-nes de tha-pa-tos
shoe polish	el betún	be-**toon**
shoes	los zapatos	tha-pa-tos
shop	la tienda	tyen-da
shopping centre	el centro comercial	then-tro ko-mair-thee-al
shore	la orilla	o-ree-llya
short	corto	kor-toh
shorts	los pantalones cortos	pan-ta-lo-nes kor-tos
show	el espectáculo	es-pek-**ta**-koo-lo

show (to)	mostrar	mos-trar
shower	la ducha	doo-cha
shut (to)	cerrar	ther-rar
shut *pp*	cerrado	ther-ra-doh
sick	enfermo	en fair-mo
side	el lado	la-doh
sights	los lugares interesantes	loo-gar-es een-tair-es-antes
sign	el letrero	le-trair-o
sign (to)	firmar	feer-mar
signature	la firma	feer-ma
silver	la plata	pla-ta
simple	sencillo	sen-thee-llyo
since	desde	des-de
sing (to)	cantar	kan-tar
single	solo	so-lo
single room	la habitación individual	abee-ta-thyos een-dee-ber-dws
sister	la hermana	air-ma-na
sit, sit down (to)	sentarse	sen-tar-se
size	el tamaño	ta-man-yo
skid (to)	patinar	pa-tee-nar
skirt	la falda	fal-da
sky	el cielo	thye-lo

sleep (to)	dormir	dor-meer
sleeper	la cama	ka-ma
sleeping bag	el saco de dormir	sa-ko de dor-meer
sleeve	la manga	man-ga
slice	la porción	por-thyon
slip	la combinación	kom-bee-na-thyon
slippers	las zapatillas	tha-pa-tee-llyas
slow	lento	len-toh
small	pequeño	pe-ken-yo
smart	elegante	ele-gan-te
smell	el olor	o-lor
smell (to)	oler	o-lair
smile	sonreír	son-re-eer
smoke (to)	fumar	foo-mar
(no) smoking	prohibido fumar	pro-ee-bee-do foo-mar
snow	la nieve	nye-be
(it is) snowing	nieva	nye-ba
so	así	a-see
sober	sobrio	so-bree-o
soap	el jabón	ha-bon
soap powder	el jabón en polvo	ha-bon en pol-bo
socks	los calcetines	kal-the-tee-nes
soft	suave	swa-be
sold	vendido	ben-dee-doh

sole *shoe*	la suela	swe-la
solid	sólido	so-lee-doh
some	algunos	al-goo-nos
somebody	alguien	alg-yen
somehow	de alguna manera	de al-goo-na ma-nair-a
something	algo	al-go
sometimes	algunas veces	al-goo-nas be-thes
somewhere	en algún sitio	en al-**goon** see-tyo
son	el hijo	ee-ho
song	la canción	kan-**thyon**
soon	pronto	pron-toh
sort	la clase	kla-se
sound	el sonido	so-nee-doh
sour	agrio	ag-ree-oh
south	el sur	soor
souvenir	el recuerdo	re-kwer-doh
space	el espacio	es-pa-thee-o
Spain	España *f*	es-pan-ya
Spanish	español	es-pan-yol
spanner	la llave inglesa	llya-be een-gle-sa
spare	disponible	dees-po-nee-ble
speak (to)	hablar	ab-lar
speciality	la especialidad	es-pe-thya-lee-da
spectacles	las gafas	ga-fas

speed	la velocidad	be-lo-thee-da
speed limit	la velocidad limitada	be-lo-thee-da lee-mee-ta-da
spend (to)	gastar	gas-tar
spring *water*	el manantial	man-an-tee-al
spoon	la cuchara	koo-cha-ra
sports	los deportes	de-por-tes
spot *stain*	la mancha	man-cha
square	la plaza	pla-tha
square *adj.*	cuadrado	kwad-ra-doh
stage	el escenario	es-then-ar-yo
stain	la mancha	man-cha
stained	manchado	man-cha-do
stairs	la escalera	es-ka-lair-a
stalls *theatre*	la butaca	boo-ta-ka
stamp	el sello	se-llyo
stand (to)	estar de pie	es-tar de pye
star	la estrella	es-tre-llya
start (to)	empezar	em-pe-thar
station	la estación	es-ta-**thyon**
statue	la estatua	es-ta-too-a
stay (to)	quedarse	ke-dar-se
steward	el mozo	mo-tho
stewardess	la camarera/la azafata	ka-ma-re-ra/a-tha-fa-ta

stick	el bastón	bas-ton
stiff	rígido	ree-hee-doh
still *not moving*	quieto	kee-e-toh
still *time*	todavía	to-da-bee-a
sting	el aguijón/	ag-ee-hon/
	la picadura	pee-ka-doo-ra
stockings	las medias	me-dyas
stolen	robado	ro-ba-doh
stone	la piedra	pye-dra
stool	el taburete	ta-boo-re-te
stop (to)	parar	pa-rar
store	la tienda	tyen-da
storm	la tormenta	tor-men-ta
stove	el infiernillo	een-fyair-nee-llyo
straight	derecho	de-re-cho
straight on	todo seguido	toh-doh se-gee-doh
strange	extraño	es-tran-yo
strap	la correa	kor-ray-a
stream	el arroyo	ar-roy-oh
street	la calle	ka-llye
stretch (to)	estirar	es-tee-rar
string	la cuerda	kwair-da
strong	fuerte	fwair-te
student	el estudiante	es-too-dyan-te

style	el estilo	es-tee-loh
subject	la tema	te-ma
suburb	el suburbio	soo-boor-byo
subway	el paso subterráneo	pa-so soob-tair-**ran**-yo
such	tal	tal
suede	el ante	an-te
suggestion	la sugerencia	soo-hair-en-thee-a
suit	el traje (de chaqueta)	tra-ha
suitcase	la maleta	ma-le-ta
sun	el sol	sol
sunbathe (to)	tomar el sol	to-mar el sol
sunburn	la quemadura de sol	ke-ma-doo-ra de sol
sunglasses	las gafas de sol	ga-fas de sol
sunhat	el sombrero de sol	som-brair-oh de sol
sunshade	el toldo	tol-doh
suntan oil	el aceite para broncear	a-thay-te pa-ra bron-the-ar
supper	la cena	the-na
supplementary charge	el suplemento	soo-ple-men-toh
sure	seguro	se-goo-ro
surgery	la clínica	klee-nee-ka
surgery hours	las horas de consulta	o-ras de kon-sool-ta
surprise	la sorpresa	sor-pre-sa

suspender belt	el liguero	lee-gair-oh
sweat	el sudor	soo-dor
sweater	el jersey	hair-say
sweet	dulce	dool-the
sweets	los caramelos	ka-ra-me-los
swell (to)	hinchar	een-char
swim (to)	nadar	na-dar
swimming pool	la piscina	pees-thee-na
swing	el columpio	kol-oom-pee-o
switch *light*	la llave de la luz	llya-be de la looth
swollen	hinchado	een-cha-do
synagogue	la sinagoga	see-na-go-ga

T

table	la mesa	me-sa
tablecloth	el mantel	man-tel
tablet	la pastilla	pas-tee-llya
tailor	el sastre	sas-tre
take (to)	tomar	toh-mar
talk (to)	hablar	ab-lar
tall	alto	al-toh
tanned	bronceado	bron-thee-a-doh

tank *reservoir*	el tanque	tan-ke
tap	el grifo	gree-fo
taste	el gusto	goos-toh
taste (to)	probar	pro-bar
tax	el impuesto (de lujo)	eem-pwes-toh
taxi	el taxi	tak-see
taxi rank	la parada de taxis	pa-ra-da de tak-see
teach (to)	enseñar	en-sen-yar
tear	la rasgadura	ras-ga-doo-ra
tear (to)	rasgar	ras-gar
telegram	el telegrama	tele-grama
telephone (to)	telefonear	tele-fo-ne-ar
telephone	el teléfono	te-le-fo-no
telephone box	la cabina telefónica	ka-bee-na tele-**fo**-nee-ka
telephone call	la llamada telefónica	llya-ma-da tele-**fo**-nee-ka
telephone directory	la lista de teléfonos	lees-ta de te-**le**-fo-nos
telephone number	el número de teléfono	**noo**-mair-oh de te-**le**-fo-no
telephone operator	la telefonista	tele-fo-nees-ta
television	la televisión	tele-bee-**syon**
tell (to)	decir	de-theer
temperature	la temperatura	tem-pair-a-too-ra
temporary	temporalmente	tem-por-al-men-te

tennis	el tenis	te-nees
tent	la tienda (de campaña)	tyen-da
tent peg	la estaquilla	es-ta-kee-llya
tent pole	el palo de la tienda	pa-lo de la tyen-da
terrace	la terraza	ter-ra-tha
than	que	ke
that	ese	e-se
theatre	el teatro	te-a-tro
their	su	soo
then	entonces	en-ton-thes
there	allí	a-llyee
there is/are	hay	'eye'
thermometer	el termómetro	tair-mo-me-tro
these	estos	es-tos
they	ellos	ellyos
thick	grueso	grwe-so
thin	fino	fee-no
thing	la cosa	ko-sa
think (to)	pensar	pen-sar
thirsty (to be)	tener sed	te-nair se
this	este	es-te
those	aquellos	ake-llyos
thread	el hilo	ee-lo
through	por	por

throw (to)	tirar	tee-rar
thunderstorm	la tormenta	tor-men-ta
ticket *train*	el billete	bee-llye-te
ticket *theatre*	la entrada	en-tra-da
tide	la marea	ma-re-a
tie	la corbata	kor-ba-ta
tight	ajustado	a-hoos-ta-doh
time	el tiempo/la hora	tyem-po/or-a
timetable	el horario	orar-yo
tin	la lata	la-ta
tin opener	el abrelatas	abre-la-tas
tip	la propina	pro-pee-na
tip (to)	dar propina	dar pro-pee-na
tired (to be)	estar cansado	es-tar kan-sa-doh
tissues *paper*	los pañuelos de papel	pan-ywe-los de pa-pel
to	a	a
toast	la tostada	tos-ta-da
tobacco (brown/ virginia)	el tabaco (negro/ rubio)	ta-ba-ko (ne-gro/ roo-byo)
tobacco pouch	la petaca	pe-ta-ka
today	hoy	oy
together	juntos	hoon-tos
toilet	los servicios	sair-bee-thyos
toilet paper	el papel higiénico	pa-pel ee-**hyen**-ee-ko

tonight	esta noche	es-ta no-che
too *also*	también	tam-**byen**
too, too much/many	demasiado	de-ma-sya-do
toothbrush	el cepillo de dientes	the-pee-llyo de dyen-tes
toothpaste	el dentífrico	den-**tee**-free-ko
toothpick	el palillo	pal-ee-llyo
top	la cima	thee-ma
torch	la linterna	leen-tair-na
torn	roto	ro-toh
touch (to)	tocar	toh-kar
tough	duro	doo-ro
tour	la excursión	eks-koor-**syon**
tourist	el turista	too-rees-ta
towards	hacia	a-thya
towel	la toalla	toh-a-llya
tower	la torre	tor-re
town	la ciudad	thyoo-da
town hall	el ayuntamiento	a-yoon-ta-myen-toh
toy	el juguete	hoo-ge-te
traffic	el tráfico	**tra**-fee-ko
traffic jam	el taponamiento	ta-po-na-myen-toh
traffic lights	las luces de tráfico	loo-thes de **tra**-fee-ko

trailer	el remolque	re-mol-ke
train	el tren	tren
tram	la tranvía	tran-bee-a
transfer (to)	trasladar	tras-la-dar
transit	tránsito	**tran**-see-toh
translate (to)	traducir	tra-doo-theer
travel (to)	viajar	bya-har
travel agent	la agencia de viajes	ahen-thee-a de bya-hes
traveller	el viajero	bya-hair-oh
traveller's cheque	el cheque de viajero	che-ke de bya-hair-oh
treat (to)	tratar	tra-tar
treatment	el tratamiento	tra-ta-myen-toh
tree	el árbol	**ar**-bol
trip	el viaje	bya-he
trouble	la dificultad	dee-fee-kool-ta
trousers	los pantalones	pan-ta-lo-nes
true	verdad	bair-da
trunk *luggage*	el baúl	ba-**ool**
trunks *bathing*	el bañador	ban-ya-dor
truth	la verdad	bair-da
try (to)	intentar	een-ten-tar
try on (to)	probarse	pro-bar-se
tunnel	el túnel	**too**-nel
turn (to)	dar la vuelta/volver	dar la bwel-ta/bol-bair
turning	la vuelta	bwel-ta

tweezers	las pinzas	pin-thas
twin beds	las camas gemelas	ka-mas he-me-las
twisted	torcido	tor-thee-doh

U

ugly	feo	fe-oh
umbrella	el paraguas	pa-ra-gwas
(beach) umbrella	la sombrilla	som-bree-llya
uncle	el tío	tee-oh
uncomfortable	incómodo	een-ko-mo-doh
under(neath)	debajo (de)	de-ba-ho
underground	el metro	me-tro
underpants	los calzoncillos	kal-thon-thee-llyos
understand	entender	en-ten-dair
underwater fishing	pesca submarina	pes-ka soob-mar-eena
underwear	la ropa interior	ro-pa een-ter-yor
university	la universidad	oo-nee-bair-see-da
unpack	deshacer las maletas	des-a-thair las ma-le-tas
until	hasta	as-ta
unusual	raro	ra-ro
up, upstairs	arriba	ar-ree-ba
urgent	urgente	oor-hen-te

us	nos	nos
U.S.A.	Estados Unidos (De América) m	es-ta-dos oo-nee-dos de a-me-ree-ka
use (to)	usar	oo-sar
useful	útil	oo-teel
useless	inútil	een-oo-teel
usual	usual	oo-soo-al

V

vacant	libre	lee-bre
vacancies	hay habitaciones	'eye' a-bee-ta-thyo-nes
vacation	las vacaciones	ba-ka-thyo-nes
valid	válido	**ba**-lee-doh
valley	el valle	ba-llye
valuable	valioso	bal-yo-so
value	el valor	ba-lor
vase	el florero	flo-rair-oh
vegetable	la legumbre	le-goom-bre
vegetarian	vegetariano	be-he-ta-rya-no
ventilation	la ventilación	ben-tee-la-**thyon**
very	muy	mwee
very little	muy poco	mwee po-ko
very much	mucho	moo-cho

vest	la camiseta	ka-mee-se-ta
view	la vista	bees-ta
villa	la villa	bee-llya
village	el pueblo	pwe-blo
violin	el violín	byo-**leen**
visa	la visa	bee-sa
visibility	la visibilidad	bee-see-bee-lee-da
visit	la visita	bee-see-ta
visit (to)	visitar	bee-see-tar
voice	la voz	both
voltage	el voltaje	bol-ta-he
voyage	el viaje	bya-he

wait (to)	esperar	es-pair-ar
waiter	el camarero	ka-ma-rair-oh
waiting room	la sala de espera	sa-la de es-pair-a
waitress	la camarera	ka-ma-rair-a
wake (to)	despertar	des-pair-tar
Wales	Gales *m*	ga-les
walk	el paseo	pa-se-oh
walk (to)	ir a pie/caminar	eer a pee-ay/ka-meen-ar

wall	la pared	pa-re
wall plug	el taco	ta-ko
wallet	el billetero	bee-llye-tair-oh
want (to)	querer	ke-rair
wardrobe	el armario	ar-mar-yo
warm *food, drink*	caliente	kal-yen-te
warm *weather*	cálido	ka-lee-doh
wash (to)	lavar	la-bar
washbasin	el lavabo	la-ba-boh
waste	el desperdicio	des-pair-dee-thyo
waste (to)	desperdiciar	des-pair-dee-thyar
watch	el reloj	re-lo-h
water (fresh/salt)	el agua *f* (dulce/salada)	ag-wa (dool-the/sa-la-da)
waterfall	la cascada	kas-ka-da
waterproof	impermeable	eem-pair-me-ab-le
water ski-ing	el esquí acuático	es-kee a-kwa-tee-ko
wave	la ola	o-la
way	el camino	ka-mee-no
we	nosotros	no-so-tros
wear (to)	llevar	llye-bar
weather	el tiempo	tyem-po
week	la semana	se-ma-na
weigh (to)	pesar	pe-sar
weight	el peso	pe-so

welcome	bienvenido	byen-be-nee-doh
well	bien	byen
Welsh	galés	ga-les
west	el oeste	oes-te
wet	húmedo	oo-me-doh
what?	¿qué?	ke
wheel	la rueda	rwe-da
when?	¿cuándo?	kwan-doh
where?	¿dónde?	don-de
which?	¿cuál?	kwal
while	mientras	myen-tras
who?	¿quién?	kyen
whole	todo	toh-doh
whose?	¿de quién?	de kyen
why?	¿por qué?	por ke
wide	ancho	an-cho
widow	la viuda	byoo-da
widower	el viudo	byoo-doh
wife	la mujer	moo-hair
wild	salvaje	sal-ba-he
win (to)	ganar	ga-nar
wind	el viento	byen-toh
window	la ventana	ben-ta-na
wing	la ala	a-la

wire	el alambre	al-am-bre
wish (to)	desear	de-se-ar
with	con	kon
without	sin	seen
woman	la mujer	moo-hair
wood	el bosque	bos-ke
wool	la lana	la-na
word	la palabra	pa-la-bra
work	el trabajo	tra-ba-ho
work (to)	trabajar	tra-ba-har
worry (to)	preocuparse	pre-ok-oo-par-se
worse	peor	pe-or
worth (to be)	valer	ba-lair
wrap	envolver	en-bol-bair
write (to)	escribir	es-kree-beer
writing paper	el papel de escribir	pa-pel de es-kree-beer
wrong	equivocado	ekee-bo-ka-doh

Y

yacht	el yate	ya-te
year	el año	an-yo
yet	todavía	to-da-**bee-a**
you	usted	oos-te
young	joven	ho-ben

your	su	soo
youth hostel	el albergue juvenil	al-bair-ge hoo-be-neel

Z

zip	la cremallera	kre-ma-llye-ra
zoo	el (parque) zoológico	par-ke thoo-o-lo-hee-ko

Index

Notes

Notes